In Search Of
MAYBERRY

A Guide To North Carolina's Favorite Small Towns

BY SCOTT DICKSON

Parkway Publishers, Inc.
Boone, North Carolina

available from:
Parkway Publishers, Inc.
Post Office Box 3678
Boone, North Carolina 28607
www.parkwaypublishers.com
Tel/Fax: (828) 265-3993

Library of Congress Cataloging-in-Publication Data

Dickson, Scott.
   In search of Mayberry / by Scott Dickson.
      p. cm.
   ISBN 1-887905-98-7
   1. North Carolina--History, Local. 2. Cities and towns--North Carolina. 3. Mayberry R.F.D.
4. North Carolina--Social life and customs. 5. City and town life--North Carolina. I. Title.

F255.D53 2004
975.6--dc22

                            2004015744

Cover Author photo by Linda Weaver; www.portraitartist.com/weaver
Book Design by Aaron Burleson, Spokesmedia

TABLE OF CONTENTS

"In the town where I was raised, the clock ticks and the cattle graze. Time passed with amazing grace, back where I come from."

– Kenny Chesney

"I was born in a small town. And I live in a small town. Hope I die in a small town. Yep, that's probably where they'll bury me."

– John Mellencamp

"May the good Lord make you smart enough to live in a small town."

– from the movie
Runaway Bride

IN SEARCH OF MAYBERRY

Introduction

While Andy Griffith may have created the mythical town of Mayberry, North Carolina for his television show, it may not actually be 100% make-believe. The small, sleepy little town, full of extremely nice people and memorable characters is a legacy that North Carolina and its people will probably never forget. In fact, most North Carolinians embrace the show and the fact that it is most likely based on Mount Airy, NC. Andy Griffith is the state's favorite son, and the town portrayed in the show is just as much a part of North Carolina as ACC Basketball, the Carolina Panthers, Grandfather Mountain, or the Cape Hatteras Lighthouse.

Millions and millions of people have watched the Andy Griffith Show since its debut on October 3rd, 1960. As my Grandfather always used to say, "You're never too old or too young to love Mayberry." As long as there are rerun watchers clubs, websites, conventions, newsletters, and countless books and documentaries dedicated to the program, Sheriff Taylor and friends will forever remain in the hearts and minds of people who long for the simpler life to return.

Folks from all over the country flock to Griffith's hometown of Mount Airy to buy merchandise and get an idea of what Mayberry might actually be like. The only difference is Mount Airy is not Mayberry. Mount Airy is an actual place, while Mayberry enjoys a fictional, almost unbelievable existence. It seems the "Old North State" of North Carolina will always be associated with Mayberry and small town living.

If you're a huge fan of The Andy Griffith Show like myself, it's safe to say that you too have once fantasized of living in a quiet little town where the living is slow & easy. So, you think those types of places don't exist? You think Mayberry is a fantasyland? Contrary to popular belief, there are dozens of beautiful little settlements in North Carolina that strongly resemble televisions' favorite small town.

Let's imagine life in Mayberry for a moment. Imagine going for a stroll down Main Street. We'll start out at Floyd's Barber Shop for a quick haircut and a chat with the boys, and then stop by the diner for a bite to eat. Next it's over to Weaver's Department Store for a bit of shopping, then next door to Walker's Drug Store for a soda. After that let's ride out to Wally's Filling Station for a bottle of pop. On our way back through town we'll go by the courthouse to see what desperate criminals ole Sheriff Taylor and Deputy Fife are hot after today. Finally, at the end of a long day we can go home to the Taylor House on Maple Street where Aunt Bee has undoubtedly fixed us a nice big supper and we can relax on the porch with a cup of coffee after dinner.

To those of us that love Mayberry, The Andy Griffith Show is more than just a TV show. It has an unmistakable appeal that satisfies the hunger in all of us to re-live or return to a time in our lives when things were simpler, easier and less stressful. It generates a feeling of being back home where we belong. It is a town where there is little to no crime (outside of moon-shining), hardly any traffic problems, no drugs on the streets, and no guns in the schools. Mayberry was a place where people could feel completely safe and comfortable.

In small towns across North Carolina people greet one another on the street by name, or honk their car horns as they drive by. Occupied storefronts line the thriving downtown districts. Tree-lined sidewalks have people strolling along. On a sunny day residents sit chatting on their front porches. Many North Carolina small towns possess a good balance between industry, agriculture & suburbia; but the real draw to these places is lifestyle. Families are finding out that knowing your neighborhood, knowing the people you go to church with, and feeling comfortable with your children playing out in the front yard are extremely important qualifications in finding a place to live. Also, one can realize the American dream of owning your own business without having to move to a big city.

In fact, small towns continue to represent all that America was founded on. Family and traditional values, neighborly people, the importance of courtesy, strong community ties, and the feeling of "being home" are part of what makes small town living so important and attractive to people in today's world. With all types of people from all walks of life searching for something better, they need look no farther than the peaceful little town just minutes away from the city limits of Charlotte, Greensboro, Raleigh, Asheville or any of the other larger cities.

How does The Andy Griffith Show manage to make us yearn for such things? Maybe it's the friendliness of the characters, the way everybody is quick to share a handshake or a neighborly shout hello. It's the constant search in all of us for something more wholesome and real. It's something that clicks in our heads and brings us back to where we came from. Perhaps it's the feeling of "being home" and at ease with the world around us. Still maybe it's something much, much more than that. People these days seem to be in search of a better way of life, but don't know where to look.

The complete and total appeal of Mayberry is something that is sure to confuse the person who has never seen the show and fallen in love with everything it stands for. In America today people tend to take the simpler things in life for granted. Large, corporate chains of stores are taking over our country and small-town local merchants are in great danger. These independently owned stores are a big part of what makes places like Mayberry so special.

Americans need to get back to a simpler way of life where cell phones, computers, emails and MTV are a thing of the past. A recent study reported that the average American spends a total of 15 years of their life watching television. Therein lies the problem. The TV shows of today compared to the ones shown from the late 50's to mid 60's are extreme polar opposites. The Andy Griffith Show is the perfect portrayal of how people should treat others. It teaches many valuable lessons from "honesty is the best policy" to "do unto others as you would have them do unto you." The show also teaches the love of family, friendship, neighbors and most of all, home. Today's TV teaches us nothing of the sort and has even more to be desired. Sure, there are a few exceptions. However, in the 50's and 60's the FCC would never allow something like "The Osbourne's," "Southpark," "Jerry Springer," or "Beavis & Butthead." At least, we'd like to think so.

We need to spend more time focusing on things like charity softball games, walks in the park and Sunday afternoon drives in the country. Thankfully, neighborhood & family gatherings with tons of fried chicken, corn on the cob, and mashed potatoes still take place in dozens of small towns right here in North Carolina. While the biggest social event of the year in Mayberry was the Founder's Day Festival, today's small towns provide state of the art recreational facilities, as well as a broad assortment of cultural activities and celebrations. These days small towns are equipped with expert medical care, higher educational opportunities and thriving neighborhood subdivisions. Also, while Mayberry only had its one underpass, all it takes is one exit off the interstate to find yourself right smack dab in the middle of a peaceful little community where the people treat you like family.

People all over this country are born and raised in "Mayberry's" and it's the only life they've ever known. These people love their small town life, but probably don't even realize how lucky they really are! One must understand that a small town mentality can only be learned or appreciated by a certain type of person. While some city folk may find it silly, there are millions of people out there who are trapped in the "city life" while they yearn for the simpler, more grounded, slower lifestyle found in the small towns of yesteryear. Fortunately, yesteryear still exists today in the rural areas of North Carolina. When new people move into these towns, neighbors get to know them real quick.

Small towns are a crucial part of the changing and evolving economy in North Carolina. The small size and scattered nature of the textile industry helps account for most of the towns in this state. In the 19th century, mills were built along rivers and creeks which gave them their power. Villages and farms then grew up around these mills. So, when electricity came along and took away the need for waterpower, these villages grew into mill towns. Pretty soon, farmers facing hard times turned to the mills for work and the towns flourished.

This rural way of life stayed strong from generation to generation, and even as North Carolina became the state with the largest percentage of its work force in manufacturing, much of the population stayed in small towns instead of clustered in cities. However, there is no way we can preserve these small towns we all love without economic growth. One of the best ways to do that is to take lessons from The Andy Griffith Show. No town could match Mayberry in charm, warmth and benevolence.

A small town can be defined as an incorporated community with a population between 2,500 and 15,000. Big enough to be more than just a few small neighborhood subdivisions, but not so big that Barney Fife would have trouble finding his way around town. There are more than 120 Tar Heel towns fitting that description. There must be a way to control the growth while keeping the small town atmosphere and setting.

During my childhood I can remember my family always watching The Andy Griffith Show. As a child I laughed my head off. But, as I grew into my teenage years I found the show to be only mildly amusing. I'd get a little chuckle when Barney would accidentally shoot off his gun, or when Otis would stumble in drunk on a Saturday night. However, I really didn't grasp that the show was more than just television comedy. By now, millions and millions of people have discovered that The Andy Griffith Show has significance and importance way past the comedic overtones.

I lived in one of those "big cities" for 6 years and experienced all the hustle and bustle it has to offer. But, I found myself thinking more and more of being back home in the little village I grew up in. I wanted to get back to basics and it was The Andy Griffith Show that brought me back to that frame of mind.

My days in that big city began with the alarm sounding promptly at 6:30 in the morning. I was usually on the couch in front of the TV, eating a bowl of cereal by 7:00. While flipping through channels one morning I came across The Andy Griffith Show. As I sat there totally enjoying the show like never before, something happened. A feeling of peace and comfort came over me and I became completely engrossed in that show.

I soon began religiously taping the show each and every morning until I had nearly ten to twelve videotapes full of Mayberry. It became a daily ritual for me. It was "must-see TV" in every sense of the word. Soon after that I was spending more of my spare time watching tapes of the program. It didn't take long for me to realize that I needed to get back home. Before I knew it I had quit my job, moved back and started working all over again. But this time it was different. I could relax around family and friends while enjoying myself and taking in all the peacefulness of being away from a big city. High school football games, backyard barbecues, and church picnics crept back into my life.

Soon after moving home I began attending the annual "Mayberry Days" festival held each September in Mount Airy. Usually there are former Andy Griffith Show cast members in attendance and the town dresses up for the occasion. It is one of the biggest weekends of the year. In addition, I was joining clubs and ordering newsletters and merchandise from stores. I was a full-blown "Mayberry addict."

I was born and raised in an area of Central North Carolina known as the Piedmont. I attended college in the North Carolina Mountains at Appalachian State University and spent countless summers on the Carolina coast and the Outer Banks. I've been to numerous college football games on beautiful Saturday afternoons in the fall. I've admired the majestic mountains of the Blue Ride, and I've enjoyed moonlit walks along the beaches of our great state. I'm extremely proud of where I'm from and what North Carolina means to me. The Dickson family history dates back to the early 1700's near the coast in Duplin County, NC. Perhaps Charles Kurault stated it best when he penned, "North Carolina is My Home."

The real purpose and inspiration of this book is to prove to people that they can actually find their own personal Mayberry not far from where they are right now. All these special places have beautiful downtown areas with local merchants and sidewalk shops. Some have more history than others, but all have a way of taking you back a few years and bringing back that nostalgic feeling of home.

When I began picking the towns I remembered someone in my family saying what a neat place Elkin was. I knew it was only an hour away from the house, so one day I grabbed my camera and went for a drive. This was in late winter and the area had just recovered from a fairly major snowfall. I reached Elkin on an early Saturday afternoon and found it quite busy with some snow left on the ground, which added scenery to my photos. Elkin is very charming and the people there were friendly, helpful and courteous. There are plenty of things to do and places to shop. I got some great pictures while visiting and found out how important Elkin is to that particular area of the state, as well as some it's fascinating history.

After I had photographed Elkin I started to explore other small towns in the state. I knew that Hillsborough had to be next. My family has roots there and I know it like the back of my hand. The weather was cloudy and rainy on the day I traveled to the town. Luckily, I completed photographing the town before any drops fell. What I captured ending up being a history lesson, along with some special moments in a town that is special to me. It's becoming more and more popular with its close proximity to Raleigh/Durham/Chapel Hill and the Research Triangle Park. Hillsborough is full of history, pride and hard-working people that really care about their town and work hard to preserve its heritage.

In the early spring I was visiting the eastern part of the state. I was excited to learn that Beaufort was less than an hour away. My aunt lived in Atlantic Beach for nearly fifteen years and our family spent quite a bit of time in that area. We made countless trips to Beaufort for delicious one-of-a-kind seafood dinners. We'd also hunt for Sinbad, the legendary figure that often graced the docks of the historic town. I visited many of the places I had known growing up and enjoyed the relaxed atmosphere of the town. Beaufort is a place rich in history, culture and colorful characters.

One beautiful attraction is the waterfront dock and walkway just across the street from the many shops and historic buildings.

While scanning the area for other towns I came across something that looked promising. Swansboro was a place I had heard of, but never researched. I soon discovered it was perfect for what I had in mind. However, not until I crossed the bridge into the downtown area did I realize what a gem I had discovered. So many shops, art galleries and antique stores line the streets of downtown. I also discovered what a historic town it is and also how friendly the local people are. It is a relaxing and peaceful place that deserves to be recognized as a wonderful tourist destination, as well as a great place to retire or raise a family. The residential area that lies just a few blocks from downtown is very charming. I was very pleased to have discovered such a fabulous new town that I knew very little about.

Visiting small towns in North Carolina would not be complete without a visit to Mount Airy. Already famous as Andy Griffith's hometown, these people have taken it a step further. This town has truly gone out of its way to embrace the feeling of down-home hospitality and community spirit. I had visited the town many times and knew exactly what I wanted to photograph. I spent that whole Saturday taking pictures. However, what I hadn't discovered were the many historic homes and buildings located just blocks away from downtown. I spent a night in Andy Griffith's childhood home, which has been converted into a bed & breakfast. I was like a kid in a candy store and was able to get some real good photographs of the town. The people there are so friendly. It feels like going home every time I venture back there.

Soon afterwards Black Mountain came to mind. I can remember going through that town as a small child. My grandparents used to take my cousin and I to Cherokee on vacation and we would pass through Black Mountain on the way. I remember one of the first things I saw when we took the exit off I-40. As we drove into town a community softball game was in full swing. I remember thinking what a testament this softball game was to small town values and ideals. Black Mountain is so scenic and full of things to do and shops to explore. There's also a real sense of community and plenty of smiling faces to go around. It was a sunny Saturday morning, so there were plenty of people in the downtown area, which added to the charming feel of the town.

Dillsboro was next in line as we ventured southwest on our trip through the North Carolina mountains. Now, I had read about Dillsboro in several magazines. I was excited to get to visit there in person. Upon arrival we found people scurrying around and shopping like crazy. Had I known there was a train there I would've made arrangements to stay longer, but I had plenty to photograph and that kept me busy. What I noticed most about Dillsboro is how incredibly clean and authentic it looks. The people in this town obviously work very hard to keep it looking as historic and authentic as possible. It was a brilliant spring afternoon, which made it very easy to photograph, and I remember enjoying a quiet picnic by the river.

I was aware of West Jefferson mostly from my days at Appalachian State University. My friends and I would go on outings just for the sake of exploring and I remembered a little bit about the town. So, early one summer Saturday morning I made my way out to the town of West Jefferson. I remembered it being quiet & peaceful that morning. The drive to the town from highway 421 is very scenic. The town is very clean with mountains all around it. The air is crisp and clear. Although there wasn't much activity in town at that time of day, it was so nice to just stroll down the sidewalks and look through the windows of all the shops and restaurants. The hardware stores, of course, were already open and hopping with business. West Jefferson has many Mayberry qualities, like the Chamber of Commerce being right in the middle of town and practically next door to the barbershop.

Davidson has always been well known mostly due to the college, but what most people don't realize is that the town is much more than just a college. It's a wonderful community with all kinds of people who love their special village and cherish every part of it. I visited Davidson late on a Saturday afternoon, and with it being early fall I was barely able to photograph the town just before the sun went down. The campus at Davidson College is breathtaking with tons of beautiful trees and impressive buildings. What I remember most is the amount of people I found sitting at tables on the sidewalks socializing, drinking coffee and reading books.

Later that fall I had a day off from work and got out a map and randomly selected an area. I got in the car and took off to Randolph County, which looked like it had some promising small towns. I was not disappointed. I literally stumbled upon Liberty just by taking the exit and following the signs. What I found was a tight-knitted community of friendly people and a town that was absolutely perfect. The area around downtown is beautifully rural with lots of rolling farmland and subdivisions. I remember walking around town, taking pictures, and being amazed at what you can discover just by taking an exit off a highway and traveling until you find something. Liberty had plenty of people doing business in the downtown area on that Wednesday. I tried to speak to as many people as I could and I made several friends that day. Liberty is in the heart of furniture country and some great furniture stores do business with customers from all over the country.

After my trip to Liberty I realized that I wanted another coastal town and a town from the middle-eastern part of the state. An opportunity came on Memorial Day weekend that next year. My family had a vacation planned and I mapped out the drive down. I picked a town in Duplin County just off I-40 on the way to Wilmington. Mount Olive turned out to be just what I was looking for. 7:30 on a Saturday morning was a little early for a stranger to be wandering the streets of downtown taking pictures in a small community. However, the people were very friendly and helpful. They pointed the way to the Mount Olive Pickle Company and on the way I discovered some beautiful historic homes. What I remember most is my wife laughing at me as I walked from street corner to street corner snapping off pictures and trying to get as much of the town on film as I could. Mount Olive is charming and quite unique. In fact, the railroad runs right through the center of town.

As we made our way down to the coast we were getting excited. We had heard so much about Southport and how amazing it was. We pulled into town and discovered the Christmas House right away. That turned out to be quite convenient because it kept my wife busy while I snuck away to explore and photograph the town. What an inspiring place Southport is. This particular Saturday afternoon was overcast and a little drizzly, but that didn't stop the countless number of tourists in town from shopping and enjoying the scenery. Southport is full of history and the downtown area is no exception with it's many historic homes and buildings. The town has a beautiful waterfront park and has entirely too many shops for you to visit in just one day. We enjoyed a delicious lunch at a seafood restaurant located on the waterway and said our goodbyes as we loaded up and headed south to be with our family.

So, whether you're looking to relocate, go for a scenic drive, or searching for a great place to vacation and shop; these twelve towns are sure to deliver exactly what you're looking for. Explore our great state and you will surely discover many hidden and not so hidden treasures...while in Search of Mayberry.

Dillsboro

Are you looking for arts & crafts, restaurants & shops, trains & movie stars? Movie stars? Yes, movie stars. All these & more can be seen in the charming mountain town of Dillsboro, NC. As a result of some major railroad and train station restorations, Dillsboro and the now famous Great Smoky Mountains Railroad have become quite popular with Hollywood producers. Movies such as This Property Is Condemned starring Robert Redford, Charles Bronson & Natalie Wood; The Fugitive with Harrison Ford & Tommy Lee Jones; My Fellow Americans starring Jack Lemmon, James Garner & Dan Aykroyd; and Forces Of Nature with Sandra Bullock & Ben Affleck; have all been filmed in the area and along the 53 miles of train track that lie between Dillsboro & Andrews, NC. Founded in 1882 when William & Alice Enloe Dills moved from nearby Webster and built a house, Dillsboro has managed to preserve many of its original buildings and all of its elegant surroundings. The Western North Carolina Railroad arrived in 1888 and Dillsboro soon became Jackson County's centerpiece of commerce. Boasting six general stores, two sawmills, two clay mines, and numerous other forms of industry, the town soon hit its peak. But by the early 1900's, three major floods nearly destroyed the town and most of the businesses moved to nearby Sylva. What's left is a perfect little town for Mayberry addicts who yearn for that simpler lifestyle; chock full of history, scenery, activities and hospitality. This quaint little village is equally famous for its shopping and mountain artistry. Stop by the Jarrett House for an old fashioned home-cooked meal or a night's lodging. Visit the original Dills House, now operating as the Well House Restaurant & Riverwood Shops. Take a stroll down Depot Street and enjoy the beautiful storefront town. Tour the local art galleries or enjoy homemade ice cream & barbecue. Shop the arts & craft stores for genuine mountain pottery. Tour the train museum, or just relax by the creek in an easy chair. All aboard for Dillsboro, the secret movie capital of North Carolina.

The famous *Great Smoky Mountains Railroad* with the *Dillsboro Depot* (shown above) is by far the most popular attraction in the area. The trains travel the fifty-three miles of track between Dillsboro and Andrews not only carrying people searching for the past, but they also carry freight to local businesses and industry. The trains are operated nearly all year long and many different options are offered concerning theme and season. There's a *Santa Express*, a *New Year's Eve Gala*, a *Dogwood Run* in the spring and a *Mystery Theatre Dinner Express* among others. Round trip excursions are available, including the Tuckasegee River, the Nantahala Gorge, the Fontana Trestle, the Red Marble Gap, a Gourmet Dinner Train, and a Raft n' Rail trip where the 22-mile train ride is followed by an 8-mile raft ride on the Nantahala River.

Dillsboro is chock full of some of the best restaurants and food in the state. Try these out: *Dillsboro Steak & Seafood*, *Dillsboro Smoke House*, *Front Street Café and Bakery*, *Huddle House Restaurant*, *New Horizons Café* and *The Well House*. For the sweet tooth don't forget *Peppermint Patti's Ice Cream and Candy Shoppe* and the *Dillsboro Chocolate Factory*.

The *Dillsboro Chocolate Factory* is famous for it's homemade chocolate creations like fudge, brittles, pralines and much more. Adding to the excitement of chocolate is the fact that you can actually watch it being made right here in the factory. Also popular at the factory are espresso, cappuccino and all kinds of gourmet foods and coffees.

The *Dillsboro Smokehouse* is well known for not only the quality of its grilled specialties but also for its quantities. Enjoy heaping amounts of hickory-smoked barbecue, including chicken, pork, beef, turkey and ribs. Housed in what appears to be an old train depot, the restaurant is highly popular and ensures a great meal.

Dillsboro is nestled in the outskirts of the Great Smoky Mountains. It's only fifteen minutes away from the entrance of the *Great Smoky Mountains National Park.* Some popular activities in the area include hiking, biking, sightseeing, the railroad, fishing, museums, golf, boating, horseback riding, skiing, and of course, shopping!

Here at the *Jackson County Visitor Information Center* you can stock up on brochures and information to help you plan your stay in Dillsboro and surrounding areas. The center provides tips on restaurants, shops of all kinds, outdoor activities, annual events, train schedules and lodging including bread and breakfasts, log cabins, hotels and more.

Perhaps one of Dillsboro's unique aspects is the convenient shopping. The merchants are all located within a few blocks of each other, which makes for easy browsing and an enjoyable shopping experience. Shoppers can also enjoy a fine meal or ice cream at one of the restaurants located only a short walk away from the stores. The train depot is also close by, which provides an escape for the guys who may not be so excited about all the shopping.

All kinds of shops thrive in Dillsboro. *Village Studio Art Gallery & Custom Framing* is popular and centrally located. The store features artwork and handcrafted gifts by local artisans and sculptors.

Southern Traditions, located across from the chocolate factory, is famous for cross-stitched items, antiques and embroidery. Like many of these charming shops, it is housed in a beautiful turn of the century home.

The *Enloe Market Place* not only resides in a historic home built in 1890 but also boasts a beautifully decorated landscape. Colors are everywhere in the spring. The store also offers a wide variety of gifts, home accessories, prints, and furniture.

If you're looking for an old-fashioned way of life, you need look no further than *Bradley's General Store.* This store offers the finest old-timey gifts and collectibles. In addition, you can step up to the old soda fountain and browse through a massive selection of t-shirts and sweatshirts.

When visiting Dillsboro visit these fine stores:

- Annie's Whim
- Cheddar Box
- CJ's
- Corn Crib
- David's Place
- Dogwood Crafters
- Front Street Co. Yarn Corner
- Gallery Z
- Heaven's Railway
- Lighten Up!
- Miss Emma's Country Store
- Mountain Pottery
- Nancy Tut's Christmas Shop
- Riverwood Craft Shop
- Riverwood Pewter Shop
- Riverwood Pottery
- Sandy's Sampler
- Shirley's Boutique
- The Crabapple Tree
- The Golden Carp
- The Nature Connection

A view of the Great Smoky Mountains Railroad as the tracks head off into the mountains. The scenic train ride begins in Dillsboro, then runs through Whittier, Bryson City, then through the Nantahala Gorge where the popular rafting river is viewed from the train, through the town of Wesser and finally stopping in Andrews. Beautiful scenery including wildlife, towns, lakes, mountains, and rivers are in abundance.

Located just down from The Jarrett House, *Maple Tree Gallery* is a popular shopping destination for pottery lovers and local artist aficionados. Dillsboro features talented local artists and their creations. Enjoy friendly hospitality and charming atmosphere in all the local galleries which includes *L. Kotila Art Gallery, Mountain Pottery, Oaks Gallery, Riverwood Pottery* and *Village Studio*.

Located all in one building, opposite the train depot, are many of the shops on Front Street. Another appealing aspect of the shops are the wraparound front porch and spectacular landscaping. Park benches are strategically placed in the shopping areas, as well as in and around Dillsboro. This is all the more encouraging for the male who would rather sit, relax and enjoy the surroundings.

After a delicious barbecue meal at the *Dillsboro Smokehouse,* walk right next door to *Yes, Dear Antiques & Gifts.* This quaint little store is located on Haywood Road, which leads to the town of Sylva and Western Carolina University. *Yes, Dear* looks like another restored train depot, but is actually a unique, warm, and inviting antique shop with a relaxing rocking-chair front porch.

A popular time to visit Dillsboro is during the Christmas season when the town is eloquently decorated in beautiful lights, ornaments and luminaries. In fact, the Dillsboro Luminaire Festival is held annually on the first and second Friday and Saturday in December.

Located at the corner of Haywood and Depot Street is the popular *Olde Towne Inn.* This historic farmhouse was converted into a bed & breakfast that boasts 4 gorgeous rooms with baths, fireplaces, ceiling fans and a picnic area. It is only a block away from the train depot.

Dillsboro offers many fine bed and breakfasts and country inns, each unique and positively charming in its own way.

Bed and Breakfasts include:

- The Applegate Inn Bed & Breakfast
- The Chalet Inn
- The Dillsboro Inn
- The Freeze House
- The Jarrett House
- The Olde Towne Inn
- Sans Souci Bed & Breakfast
- The Squire Watkins Inn

Above is a view from the train depot of Front Street and some of the shopping opportunities. Despite three major floods, Dillsboro has managed to keep many of its original buildings in good shape. Smiling faces are everywhere in this quiet mountain town where tourism and courteousy go hand in hand.

Built in 1882 by William Dills, founder of the town; *The Jarrett House* is perhaps one of the most popular country inns and restaurants in western North Carolina. Featured in *Southern Living, Our State Magazine, Friends, Eastern Airlines, the Raleigh News & Observer, the Charlotte Observer, the Winston-Salem Journal, the New York Times, the Atlanta Journal, the Chicago Tribune, the Los Angeles Times, and the Miami Herald. The Jarrett House* is also listed on the *National Register of Historic Places.* Bought by the Hartbarger Family in 1975, the inn serves up some of the finest home cooking in one of the oldest inns in the western part of the state. According to a family spokesperson, the restaurant continues to serve the home-style food, family style service and inside accommodations that the inn is famous for. Characterized by decorative porches that accommodate the countless number of rocking chairs and a scenic view of the town, the *Jarrett House* is a step back in time that encourages a relaxing and peaceful visit to the town that made it famous.

Black Mountain

Nestled on the edge of the Blue Ridge Mountains and right off Interstate 40 is a remarkably quaint little town of around 10,000. Nicknamed "The Front Porch of Western North Carolina," Black Mountain has worked hard to preserve its heritage and environment through the help of nonprofit groups and local volunteering citizens who care about their town. Evangelist Billy Graham, probably the town's most well known citizen, built his training center "The Cove" nearby and former NBA Star and UNC grad, Brad Dougherty also hails from this small mountain community. The Cherokee Indians were the first to inhabit this area. Unfortunately they were forced westward in the late 1700's as settlers looked toward the forests for hunting wild game. In 1850 a road was built through the area, and the railroad arrived in 1879. Incorporated in 1893 and voted the "Best Small Town In Western North Carolina" recently by the readers of Asheville's *Citizen Times*, Black Mountain features everything the Mayberry connoisseur could possibly wish for. The town boasts all the amenities including numerous Bed and Breakfast Inns, campgrounds, over 27 handmade craft shops, antique malls, blacksmiths, glass artists, dulcimer makers, all kinds of restaurants, trout fishing, biking, golf courses, colleges, a restored Old Railroad Depot featuring 75 crafters, and a hardware store founded in 1927 that has virtually everything you can possibly think of. Perhaps the most impressive characteristic of Black Mountain is the scenery. Beautiful mountains surround the town. Mount Mitchell, the highest peak East of the Mississippi is just a few miles away. In the fall, tourists flock to the area for conferences, festivals, recreation & sightseeing. Local folks are always happy to oblige with a smile and a "hello there." Enjoy the mountain music of a street musician yodeling and playing some bluegrass on the banjo, or sample some of the finest home-cooked cuisine this side of Aunt Bee's kitchen. Whether you're passing through town or searching for some down-home mountain hospitality,

Black Mountain is a joy you won't soon forget.

Music is a tradition that has been passed down through the years amongst the residents of Black Mountain. Bluegrass music in particular, is an important part of the town's culture, as well the entire mountain region of the state. Many hoedowns and square dances take place here in the music hall located in the downtown area.

Black Mountain's elevation is approximately 2,400 feet above sea level. This ensures summers without massive amounts of humidity and winters that are slightly on the chillier side. Outdoor activities are in abundance including hiking, boating, fishing, golf, tennis, canoeing and of course, shopping. The center of activity for outdoor activity in Black Mountain is the popular Lake Tomahawk. Lake Tomahawk offers many recreational options, including a community hall, tennis courts, a walking trail, a beautiful garden, a pool, a picnic area and of course a lake stocked full of fish just begging to be caught. Several concerts are held on the grounds throughout the course of the year.

Located on East State Street in Historic Downtown is the *Black Mountain Chamber of Commerce*. Brochures on area activities such as Mount Mitchell, restaurants, accommodations & shops are available.

The main commerce strip in downtown, Cherry Street provides a wide variety of shops, scenery and that feel of being in Downtown Mayberry. It's hard to believe that a place this captivating and relaxing could be so easy to get to.

Black Mountain has many significant annual events including the Black Mountain Marathon and Mt. Mitchell Challenge, "Taste of Black Mountain", 4th of July Celebration, the Sourwood Festival and Fall by the Tracks. To kick off the holiday season, the town holds its yearly Pumpkin Festival towards the end of October. The night before Thanksgiving is an extra special treat when all the shops downtown stay open late for Thanks-evening. Then the town is skillfully decorated for Christmas, all decked out in lights and ornaments. Norman Rockwell's paintings definitely come to mind. The Christmas season is filled with activities including a parade, the Circle of Lights at Lake Tomahawk, and a holiday tour of the local country inns.

Life in the town of Black Mountain is slow paced and relatively carefree. The town is surrounded by tall, majestic mountains and is kept very clean and decorated.

ANDRÉ MICHAUX
French botanist, pioneer in studying flora of western North Carolina, visited Black Mountains, August, 1794.

Once a prominent stopping place for railroads carrying passengers and freight, *The Old Train Depot* has been turned into an arts and crafts gallery and is the setting of the "Fall By the Tracks" celebration each October. The area boasts eight major church conference centers including, *Blue Ridge Assembly, Montreat, Camp Dorothy Walls, In the Oaks, Christmount Assembly, Cragmount Assembly, Ridgecrest and The Cove,* also known as the *Billy Grham Training Center.*

The local merchants here in Downtown Black Mountain work hard to keep the town authentic, free of pollution and clean. The area is full of all kinds of shops including art and framing galleries, antique stores, hardware stores, bookstores, specialty shops, craft shops, furniture, & clothing and jewelry stores. One of the nicest things about Black Mountain is the smiling face you get from the people who live here. The pride in their heritage & their love for Black Mountain is readily apparent in their generosity and hospitality. Mountain friendliness feels good when you're a stranger in town searching for a benevolent mountain area Mayberry. Many descendants of the early settlers in this valley still live in Black Mountain. Mountain streams provide the drinking water for the majority of the residents in this area.

Black Mountain is a family-oriented community where people get together and enjoy good times. A youth softball game on a Saturday morning ranks very high on the list of priorities for the week.

Garrou Pottery is a popular gallery in town where local and regional artists are featured. The area is rich in the arts and many local artisans showcase their talents on a regular basis. Other notable galleries include *Backtracks Gallery, Black Mountain Iron Works, Catawba Sunrise Gallery, Cherry Street Gallery, Jan's Dollhouse, Visions of Creation, Hands On Gallery, The Paint Spot & Gift Gallery, Seven Sisters Gallery, The Ginko Tree Gallery,* and the *Black Mountain Center for the Arts.*

Step back in time at the *Cherry Tree Corner Ice Cream & Soda Shop.* It's a 1950's theme, which brings to mind bobby socks, saddle oxfords and hot rods. This truly unique and fun place to eat has a checkerboard floor, fifties style stools and tables; and of course, a jukebox full of Elvis tunes. The menu offers eighteen flavors of amazing ice cream, milkshakes, floats, malts and sundaes, popcorn, freshly squeezed lemonade, all sorts of soda pop and homemade fudge. In addition, it carries a vast array of candy including wax bottles with syrup in them, wax lips, mary-jane's and Beeman's or Teaberry Gum. To top it all off, there's a karaoke machine for those who fancy themselves as entertainers. This place is not to be missed on your visit to Black Mountain. The town also has an overabundance of fine restaurants featuring all types of cuisine including *Coach House Seafood, Duck's Hot Dogs, the Green Light Café, Berliner Kidl German Restaurant, Black Mountain Bakery, Campfire Steak Buffet, My Father's Pizza, 19th Hole Snack Shop, Old Appalachian Barbecue, Olympic Flame Pizza, The Dripolator Coffeehouse, The French Quarter Café, The Front Porch Grill, Pepper's Deli, Sweatreat's,* and *Veranda's Café.*

Majestic mountain vistas provide a splendid backdrop for the *Old Train Depot*. The massive scenery surrounds the town and offers the feeling of being in a small village deep in a valley. Walking off lunch is a great way to enjoy every aspect of beautiful Black Mountain.

The beautiful little brick buildings that house the stores on Cherry Street are wonderfully decorated. Dogwood trees, flowers and benches line the sidewalks. This is obviously provided for those who'd rather sit and enjoy the mountain air and scenery.

The shops in Downtown Black Mountain are plentiful, including *Mountain Valley Clothing Store* and *New Century Metalsmith Shop* (above). The downtown area has many gift shops, each equally quaint and charming. These include *Bramblewood Cottage, The Emporium, the McCosh House, Marti's Patchwork Cottage, Brandon's Gifts & Crafts* and *Veranda's Gift Shop*. The area wouldn't be complete without a barbershop and this town doesn't disappoint with the *Around Town Barber & Style. Howard's Antiques* has all kinds of artifacts and collectibles and *Second Look Books, Indigo Sky Book Store* and *Talespinner Books & Music* offer up all kinds of books & magazines.

Downtown Black Mountain is blessed with an unbelievable store where you can find everything you could possibly need. *Town Hardware & General Store* carries everything from lamps to lawnmowers, toys to telephones and candles to cameras. What's more, you're welcomed by a smiling face and a "May I help you?" as soon as you walk through the door. Housed in a historic brick building, the store is centrally located in the downtown area and adds to the down-home feeling you get when you

visit Black Mountain. People congregate here in the store to say hello and talk about their day and maybe their plans for that weekend. Conversations about chores and "honey-do's" are common as people come in looking for a plunger to unclog a sink, or a certain color of paint for the living room. It truly gives you the feeling of being at home in a family-oriented and friendly community.

Views like this are common and the people are wonderful. There are many bed & breakfasts to discover. These include *Black Mountain Inn, Friendship Lodge, The Inn on Mill Creek, The Monte Vista, Mote's Mountain View, The Red Rocker Inn, The Inn Around The Corner, The Renee Allen House* and *Tree Haven Bed & Breakfast.* Cabin rentals? No problem. Try *Black Mountain Cabins, Cabin Creek Lodge, High Rock Cottage & Kinkade Cottage.*

Right up the road from downtown is the *Black Mountain Public Library* where families gather to read to children and people come to do research or to just sit & relax with a favorite magazine.

The library is also a popular place for history seekers. Books describing the beginnings of the town, the mountains, the area and region and North Carolina in general can be found in the Black Mountain Public Library. Black Mountain also has charming neighborhoods, expert medical care and banks. It's a popular place for tourists, as well as families relocating and recent retirees.

West Jefferson

Neatly tucked away about 25 miles Northeast of Boone is the small, but important settlement of West Jefferson. One of only 3 incorporated towns in Ashe County; West Jefferson boasts some truly beautiful scenery while still accommodating the shopper and artist in all of us. Up until the year 1914, the town was merely a small village with only a few stores. But when the railroad arrived, things changed and West Jefferson grew into its present-day "Mayberry-style" setting rather quickly. A hotel was built, a barber shop opened, craft shops, art galleries and hardware stores came to life, and soon West Jefferson was a thriving small town with the Blue Ridge Mountains providing the background. Ashe County was settled in 1755 and was organized in 1799. The legendary Daniel Boone is heralded as one of the county's most famous hunters. In fact, Boone's ancestors were some of the first people to own land in the area. The famous New River is a big attraction in the area. The second oldest river in the world (second only to the Nile) attracts kayakers, canoe enthusiasts and rafters, as well as the avid trout fisherman. Agriculture is big, in and around West Jefferson. Major crops include tobacco, beans, apples, feed corn, hay and Christmas trees. Yes, Christmas trees. The area has over 9 million trees. 700 local farmers made more than $20 million for the local economy in 1997 alone. Chances are, the tree you bought at the nursery in your town came straight from West Jefferson and Ashe County. West Jefferson is home to North Carolina's only cheese factory as well as many wonderful restaurants specializing in home style, or down-home cooking. Stroll the downtown area to find gift shops, art galleries; hardware stores that beckon from years gone by and several antique stores. Bed and breakfasts, cabins, chalets, country inns, golfing resorts and campgrounds are in abundance for people looking for that perfect mountain getaway. Not to mention the beautiful Blue Ridge Parkway is just a hop, skip & a jump away.

Downtown West Jefferson sits in a valley with beautiful mountain scenery all around. Art galleries, hardware stores, barbershops, gift shops, antique stores and more all enjoy this peaceful little community. There is strong mutual respect that exists among its residents.

Nestled in the far northwestern corner of North Carolina, West Jefferson and Ashe County have the unique distinction of being bordered not only by the picturesque counties of Alleghany, Wilkes & Watauga but also by the states of Virginia & Tennessee. *The Ashe County Visitors Center* is the most important initial destination. There you will find helpful information on bed & breakfasts, attractions, shopping and dining.

Before explorations and settlements by the Europeans, the Creek, the Shawnee and the Cherokee Indians inhabited this land. Archaeological discoveries have led scientists to believe that wars were often fought over hunting grounds in what is now West Jefferson and Ashe County.

OK, so maybe there's not a whole lot of activity at 6:45AM on a Saturday. However, West Jefferson's beauty and charm still shine through. Historic and colorful brick buildings with clean sidewalks are professionally decorated with plants, flowers and shrubs. The mountains in the background give the town such a wonderful atmosphere and relaxing feeling.

Shops of all kinds thrive in the downtown area. *Bill & Penny's Antiques & Collectibles* is a quaint little shop full of all kinds of pottery, furniture and more. The shop is located in the old *West Jefferson Hotel*, which has been converted into a building used for retail shops, restaurants and offices.

The old *Parkway Cinema* is still in use. Many people regularly flock to the downtown area for a good meal and a good movie. In Ashe County nearly 38% is farmland and towns. The remaining 62% is forest and wilderness, of which 98% is privately owned. Looking to build a dream house in the mountains? Land is abundant and perfect in West Jefferson and Ashe County.

The *Ashe Arts Center* holds many exhibitions of arts including painting, pottery and mountain crafts. The arts center helps draw people from around the county to the beautiful downtown area in West Jefferson.

The school system here scores way above average each year. While the system maintains a low dropout rate, it is important to note that they spend more on students than the North Carolina average. Students here also score well above the average on the SAT test. In addition, top-quality medical facilities are available, as well as financial institutions, churches and civic organizations.

As North Carolina's only cheese plant, you can actually see cheese being made here in Downtown West Jefferson at the *Ashe County Cheese Company*. In business since 1930, the company also operates a gift shop and, of course, you can select from a wide variety of cheeses to purchase. Another popular attraction is the Churches of the Frescoes minutes away in neighboring Glendale Springs. Popular artist Ben Long painted frescoes in St. Mary's church and in Holy Trinity church in 1974 and 1980. People from all walks of life come from all over the nation to view these amazing pieces of work.

Perhaps West Jefferson and Ashe County is most widely known as the Christmas Tree capital of the world. Every year thousands upon thousands of trees are harvested for decorating at Christmas. In fact, the White House itself places an order for a tree from here practically every year. *Lee's Trees* in the Beaver Creek area provides a vast array of trees and sizes to choose & cut on your own.

West Jefferson has so many wonderful places to sample fine cuisine. For family-style food, *Greenfield Restaurant* offers gorgeous views from Mt. Jefferson Road and a rocking chair front porch. Other notables include the *Lansing Restaurant, The Tea Room, Havana Grill, S&S Mini Mart, Winner's Circle Steak House, Smokey Mountain Barbecue, The Three Bears, Shatley Springs, Smithey's Restaurant* and *the Garden Gate Café*.

Few things are as special as a good old-fashioned hardware store. *W.J. Hardware* is exactly that. Other fine stores include: *Ray Hardware Co., Skyland Books, Beth Ball Interiors, McNeill's Department Store, Whitetop Laurel Fly Shop, The Old Hotel Antiques & Collectibles, Burgess Furniture Store, The Shepherd's Staff, Josh-Rene's Treasures,* and *Sugar 'n' Spice*, to name a few.

The Old Hotel, Skyland Books and *Beth Ball Interiors* are a few of the many fine retail stores on Main Street in West Jefferson. The buildings are decorated in many colors and styles.

The *DePree Studio and Art Gallery,* located on Main Street, specializes in original art from local and regional artists. It focuses on Blue Ridge Mountain themes and also carries prints, note cards and Persian Art. Be sure to visit all the art galleries including *Ashe Custom Framing & Gallery, The Acorn Gallery* and *The Quilt Gathering,* where all your quilting needs are met.

There are plenty of things to do in West Jefferson. Hiking, biking, golf at *Mountain Aire Golf Club,* canoeing, rafting and shopping are just some of the things to keep you busy. Perhaps the best way to take it all in is through the *Lost Province Tours.* These are tours offered to charter buses, church, civic & school groups and private car tours for small groups. They can arrange accommodations for you, take you on sightseeing tours to the *New River & Blue Ridge Parkway,* and tell you the best places to eat.

Above is one of the many absolutely gorgeous views of the *New River*. The river itslef is widely believed by scientists to be the second oldest river in the world. Also, it is one of the few to travel south to north. The *New River* flows right through West Jefferson & Ashe County, creating spectacular scenery and opportunities for outdoor activities.

Accommodations are plentiful in this charming mountain community. Bed & breakfasts include *West Jefferson Bed & Breakfast, The Buffalo Tavern, the French Knob Inn, Li'l Red*

Hen Bed & Breakfast, the River House Inn, the Tobin Farm Inn, the River Farm Inn, Glendale Springs Inn and *The Gathering Place*. Cabins and chalets can also be rented through *Blue Ridge Mountain Realty, Carolina Mountain Properties* and *Deerwood Creek Park Cabins*. Several motels are available if you're not into "roughing it" including the *Park View Tourist, Nation's Inn, Best Western* and *the Highlander Motel*. Finally, there are resorts close by including *Fleetwood Falls* and *Jefferson Landing*. There's something for everyone in West Jefferson.

Mount Olive

Located just south of Goldsboro and a mere stone's throw from I-40, this peaceful little town known as Mount Olive owes its beginnings to the railroad. When the Wilmington and Weldon Railroad was completed in 1840, the foundation had been laid for what was to follow. In 1853 a post office and a train depot were erected and soon a man named Benjamin Oliver built a store nearby in Duplin County. Although Oliver is refuted to have come up with the town's name, it was his son-in-law who is believed to be the founder of Mount Olive. Oliver's son-in-law, Dr. Gideon Monroe Roberts, purchased the land around the depot and in 1854 sold four acres to Oliver and four other local men. These people laid out the town, which was incorporated in 1870 as Mount Olive. Throughout the years agriculture has been the main industry in the town. In the early 1900's Mount Olive was known as the strawberry capital of the world. But, you may be more familiar with the name from their most famous industry, pickles. *The Mount Olive Pickle Company*, established in 1926 and located just outside downtown, holds their annual "Pickle Festival" each year that draws tourists from all over the nation. The festival is held annually on the last full weekend of April. Included in this two-day pickle extravaganza are a live concert, a parade, carnival rides, art exhibits, a pancake breakfast, food vendors and an impressive fireworks display at the end of the day. Mount Olive offers every amenity needed for wonderful, laid-back, small town living. The downtown area is lined with hardware stores, furniture and antique stores, fine restaurants, gift shops, florists, historic churches and theaters, drug stores dating to the turn of the century, and running right smack through the middle of Center Street is of course, the railroad. Walk down a side road from downtown and you will discover some of the most magnificently restored historic homes in this part of the state. Included in this collection are the *Southerland-Burnette House*, which dates to 1920 (inside of which lies a much older building), *The Oaks* dating back to 1850, and the *J.A. Westbrook* house dating to 1885. The Mount Olive parks and recreation department operates two city parks, an athletic field, and is home to *Mount Olive College* which was founded by a group of Southern Baptists. The town's motto is "We Value Hometown Tradition" and it's no surprise that the peaceful, slower, relaxing lifestyle we all so desperately long for is alive and well in Mount Olive.

Waller Hardware operates right off Center Street, which allows people to do more business in the downtown area. Mount Olive has some of the finest hardware stores in the county including *Number One Builders Supply Company* and *Simmons Hardware*.

The Mount Olive storefronts vary in size and material, but all are typical of early 20th century architecture. The railroad carries freight and passengers and is still important to the town. 7:49 on a Saturday morning is a little early for downtown to be hopping, but it doesn't take long after that for things to be jumping with activity.

The town of Mount Olive was named after the Biblical "Mount of Olives." A downtown walking tour is sponsored by the *Chamber of Commerce* and is a fantastic way to visit all the landmarks. The tour includes churches, businesses, historic homes, monuments and much more. Thanks to the *Mount Olive Historical Society* the area is now on the *National Register of Historic Places*. Other civic-minded local organizations include the *Boys & Girls Club, Carver Alumni Association, Exchange Club of Mount Olive, Mount Olive Lions Club* and *The Mount Olive Rotary Club*.

The first thing that most likely comes to mind when Mount Olive is mentioned is pickles. There is, of course, the Pickle Festival each year. Then there's the pickle company itself. The company started modestly back in 1926 as just a brining company, which didn't work out the way it was planned. After going back to the drawing table, the owners decided to go for it and become a full-fledged pickle producing company. Today the *Mount Olive Pickle Company* is the largest independent pickle company in the country. Their products are shipped as far north as New Hampshire, as far south as Florida, and as far west as Texas and Oklahoma. It operates on approximately 90 acres of land not far from downtown and is housed in over 800,000 square feet of production, warehouses and offices. The company established one of the very first profit sharing plans for its employees way back in 1943. The Mount Olive Pickle Company goes through more than 100 million pounds of cucumbers each year and sells more than 80 million jars of pickles, relishes and peppers.

Located within walking distance of Downtown Mount Olive is one of the many elegant historic homes. *The DuBrutz English House* was built around 1900. This Queen Anne Style home is immaculate and gorgeous. Many of these houses are featured on the walking tour that takes you all through the town.

The *Mount Olive* Tribune is an important part of life in the town. The paper has been in business since 1904 and highly regarded by the people of this town. The population in the downtown area is approximately 5000 and nearly 35,000 within a ten-mile radius. People from outlying farms and rural communities make their way to downtown to take care of business and socialize with friends.

Whether it's to pick up something at the drug store, shop for clothing, or grab a bite of lunch, the people of Mount Olive are proud of their town, its history and their unique sense of community.

The Mount Olive Florist takes care of the floral needs like weddings and funerals, but also is well equipped with gifts and accessories. The downtown area and its storefronts are made up of unique and decorative architecture. Buildings over 100 years old are pleasing to the eye and interesting to the studious architect and scholar.

Located on Main Street in the downtown area is an incredible stately looking manor known as *The Perry-Cherry House*. This house was built in the 1930's and is a replica of an earlier nineteenth century structure. Note the extraordinary columns and cylindrical roofing addition. The home was built by Daniel Perry in the late 1890's and was sold in the early 1930's to L.G. Geddie, one of the original founders of the Mount Olive Pickle Company. Geddie, in turn, sold the house to C.S. Cherry in 1937. Other famous historic homes featured in the Mount Olive walking tour include *the Farrior- Wooten House, the Southerland-Burnette House, the Flowers-Wooten-Holmes House, The Oaks, the John Bell House, the W.F. Martin House, the D.J. Aaron House, the J.A. Westbrook House, the Cullen Hatch House, The Elms, the T.M. Rivera House, the Kornegay House, the Faison Witherington House* and one simply known as *Rick's House*. All these and much more can be enjoyed on the wonderful *Mount Olive Walking Tour.*

To honor Mount Olive's World War I veterans and to preserve its heritage, the townspeople erected this beautiful monument. Located on Center Street in the heart of downtown, the monument was dedicated in 1920. It features a water fountain on one side and a horse-watering trough on the other. Horse-drawn carriages were common in this area eighty years ago. However, these days the monument is merely a source of pride and honor for the families of those lost in the war.

Several larger metropolitan areas like Goldsboro, Kinston and Wilmington are not far away from Mount Olive. Mount Olive is a perfect place for people to live and raise a family. Some of the notable companies in Mount Olive include *Carolina Turkeys, Georgia-Pacific Corporation, IMPulse NC, the Mount Olive Pickle Company* (of course) and *Sonoco High Density Film Products.*

This impressive structure located on James Street is known as the *First United Methodist Church.* The church was organized in 1870. This particular church was built in 1913 and was designed by Henry Bonitz, an architect from Wilmington. Note the Gothic influence and the tall, impressive towers.

Especially For You, a gift shop located in downtown, is filled with specialty items such as frames, wrought iron, lamps and cards. There is also an antique store and several furniture stores including *Bobby Denning Furniture, W. R. Jennette Furniture Co., Inc., John Patterson Furniture Co. and Southern Furniture & Interiors. Peeble's Department Store* is a local favorite and popular clothing stores include *Hi-Lite's and Hi-Ho.*

It took a little while to get this picture as there were so many people coming in and out of this drug store. Even at eight o'clock on Saturday morning, this place was hopping. The unique sign was added to the building in 1950 to give the building a little flair. W.E. Lewis started the *Mount Olive Drug Company* in 1917 and it has been a hotbed of local activity ever since. Another notable drug store of equal importance in downtown Mount Olive is *Glenn Martin's Rexall Drugs.* Located beside the local florist, it too is a busy place.

Mount Olive has many fine restaurants sure to please any appetite. Some notable ones include *Andy's Cheesesteaks & Cheeseburgers, The Brokerage Restaurant, Lighthouse Family Restaurant, Nino's Italian Restaurant, Pizza Village, Steve's Pizza Place* and *Southern Belle Restaurant,* where you can always find a large group of regulars serving themselves coffee.

Liberty

Tucked away just off I-85, about 20 miles South of Greensboro is the attractive and historical town of Liberty, NC. Located near the geographic center of the state, Liberty began as a crossroads on the farm owned by Abram Brower in pre-Revolutionary War days. The town itself is named after a group of patriots who regained their freedom at the close of the War. This 1,500-acre tract originally belonged to the Lords and Proprietors Grant from Charles II of England in 1663. Churches date back to the time when the land was settled in the mid-1750's and there are references to a town called "Liberty" in transactions dating back to 1809. In the late 1800's the town was known as an educational center, much in part to the beginning of the Liberty Academy in 1886. Soon the railroad came to town and the small village prospered. Today Liberty boasts many industries including furniture, hosiery, apparel, textiles and prefabricated buildings. With about 2,000 people living in the town limits, the downtown area is comprised of fabulous antique shops, ice cream shops, restaurants, good old-fashioned hardware stores, jewelry, book and furniture stores. One of the main attractions in the downtown area is the one and only *Liberty Jubilee*. Once an old theatre, the opry house is now home to country, gospel and bluegrass music, as well as comedy stage shows and dancing. Calling itself "a real down-to-earth showplace of the Southeast with a seating capacity of nearly 500 in a smoke-free, air conditioned Theatre with plush seats, unique concessions, a gift shop, and clean family entertainment," the *Liberty Jubilee* is not to be missed. Outside the town limits you will find a population of about 10,000 living within a five-mile radius in a beautiful rural setting. The town supports a public library, an activities center, a summer recreation program, parks complete with picnic areas, ball fields and tennis courts, and many civic and fraternal organizations. *The North Carolina Zoo* in Aseboro is less than 30 minutes away. In addition, Liberty proudly features Liberty Elementary School, Northeastern Randolph Middle School, doctors of all kinds, insurance and real estate agencies and banks.

Liberty is very much a town where family values and a sense of community run deep within the character of its citizens. The storefronts in the downtown area bring back a feeling of late-fifties or early-sixties. However, with new schools, neighborhoods & subdivisions, medical facilities, financial institutions and retirement communities being built, Liberty is growing much like other small towns in North Carolina located within 30 miles of a big city.

The Chamber of Commerce stays busy in Liberty. With the rapid growth and urban sprawl of nearby cities like Greensboro and Asheboro, Liberty has proven to be a pleasant change of pace for families who want a more laid-back and relaxing atmosphere in which to live. Thriving subdivisions and family-style homes and neighborhoods are being built all around this wonderful little town.

Over 150 antique dealers flock to this small North Carolina town twice a year to celebrate the "Liberty Antiques Festival." Held in April and September, the festival is known as one of the largest antiques events in the Southeast. *Liberty Antiques*, one of many antique stores in the town, is cleverly housed in the same building as *Liberty Ice Cream Parlor.*

Liberty is also known as one of the first places that European settlers came to in pre-Revolutionary days.

Music is a popular pastime in the town of Liberty. In addition to the *Liberty Jubilee* is the wildly popular *Fiddler's Cove.* Located on Raleigh Street in the downtown area, *the Cove* features authentic, traditional bluegrass and gospel music. Local musicians, proud of their roots and heritage, expertly perform for large crowds every weekend. Audiences travel from all over the area to witness real people playing real music from their past.

A view down one of the side streets in Downtown Liberty allows us a view of the architecture, which dates back to early 1900's.

Book shops, antique shops, furniture stores, old fashioned hardware stores and jewelry stores are all part of the quaint little downtown area in Liberty. With a police force numbering less than fifteen, it ain't Mayberry, but it's pretty dog-gone close.

A popular shop to visit is *Jennie's Flower Shop* located on North Asheboro Street. Founded in 1934, this beautiful flower shop has occupied the same location since its beginning. Professional horticulturists and floriculturists take your order and the staff takes great pride in its customer service.

Not much is left of the old train depot in Liberty. The railroad gave life to this town over a hundred years ago. Although service is still available through Norfolk Southern, it is mostly used for freight & industry.

In almost every small town there's a particular type of store where you can find virtually anything and everything. Downtown Liberty is no exception. *Martin Appliance Company* (above), located on Swannanoa Avenue, has been in business for more than forty years. Considering the competition from large retailers, this charming and convenient store has stood the test of time and continues to be a major attraction to the town. It has been said that people come from neighboring towns like Siler City and Asheboro just to take advantage of this truly incredible store. Now on the *National Register of Historic Places*, the downtown area is poised to grow and renovate. There are several retail spaces for sale and the town has high expectations that the area will continue to become more and more popular. With neighborly, friendly & smiling faces everywhere you go and all the necessary amenities close by, there's no doubt whatsoever that Liberty will soon experience a major push in tourism and commerce.

North Carolina is famous worldwide for its furniture manufacturing. In fact, many towns neighboring Liberty are considered to be the furniture capitals of the world. Places such as High Point, Lexington & Thomasville are synonymous with furniture. So, it's no surprise that Liberty also has several impressive furniture stores like *The Dodge House* and *The Furniture Barn*. Furniture is also one of the twenty most important industries in Liberty.

One of the most popular restaurants in Liberty is *Fran's Front Porch*. Serving all kinds of Southern-style home-cooked meals, this beautiful dining place is set inside a restored old country farmhouse. What makes it even more unique is the fact that it is located less than 500 yards away from the Causey Airport in Liberty.

Liberty is a close-knit, family community in every sense of the word. A large percentage of the population work right here at the local manufacturing plants. There are several fine manufacturers in Liberty including *Collier-Keyworth, The Chair Company, Gregson Furniture, Kinro, Michel Thomas, Superior Components, Ultra Craft* and *Worcester Controls.*

Events such as the annual *Fall Festival,* held in October, are important to a community like Liberty. Friends, family and a small town way of life make this place a popular destination for tourists, retirees and families relocating from out of town. A popular bed & breakfast in Liberty is known as *The Inn at Rising Meadow Farm.* Located out on Williams Dairy Road, this old farmhouse and homestead now serves as perhaps one the most popular privately owned inns in this part of the state.

The famous *Liberty Jubilee* is located in Liberty on highway 49 as you come into the downtown area. Their self-described motto is "Family-Friendly Musical Shows," and quite appropriate. Country music stage shows happen every Saturday night featuring traditional country, bluegrass and gospel music. In addition, a group of national hall of fame champion cloggers perform at the venue. The jubilee is a historic theatre converted to this showplace with a seating capacity of more than 500. It also features a dance floor for those who enjoy toe tapping.The house band is called *The Jubilee Jukebox Band* and features the finest local vocalists and musicians. The *Liberty Jubilee* is widely known as clean, family entertainment at its finest. Also, the venue is available for rental for weddings, private events, etc. It is an attraction not to be missed.

Hillsborough

One of the most historically significant towns in North Carolina, Hillsborough was an important focal point of both the Revolutionary and Civil War. The town served as the capital city in colonial times and was the scene of several dramatic events including the War of the Regulation (1768-1771), the Third Provincial Congress (1775) & the raising of the Royal Standard by General Cornwallis in 1781. During the Civil War General Joseph E. Johnston called Hillsborough his temporary headquarters and from there he rode out to surrender the largest Confederate Army to General Sherman in 1865. Hillsborough was also the final residence of William Hooper, one of the signers of the Declaration of Independence, whose grave can be seen in the cemetery of the First Presbyterian Church on Tryon Street. The town was laid out and founded in 1754 by William Churton, an agent for the Earl of Granville, John Carteret. Located right in the middle of the I-85 & I-40 junction, and just a few miles west of Raleigh-Durham's Research Triangle Park, Hillsborough has lots to offer the tourist and the daily commuter. In town one can experience restaurants of all kinds, antique shops, walking tours, historic attractions and museums. The *Colonial Inn* has been offering overnight accommodations and good, old Southern home-cooked meals since 1759. The one and only George Washington even spent a night in the inn. The charming and shaded downtown area is home to numerous quaint little shops, coffeehouses and cafes, fine restaurants and jewelry stores. Visit the Alexander Dickson house (Orange County Visitors Center and Hillsborough Chamber of Commerce) to load up on information about the area and local attractions. Browse through the Orange County Historical Museum and see some of the relics and artifacts collected throughout this very special town's history, and visit the recently reconstructed Indian village by the Eno River. One of Hillsborough's most unique events is the Christmas Candlelight Tour, when these restored, historic homes and buildings dress up for the holidays and open their doors to the public, complete with tour guides fitted in colonial attire. Other special occasions include the Spring Historic Home & Garden Tour and Hillsborough Hog Day, one of the Southeast's top 20 early summer events. You don't want to miss Hillsborough.

The Colonial Inn (above). Though the current inn was expanded upon a tavern built in 1838, it is said that a tavern has stood here since 1759. *Cornwallis* himself paved the streets with flagstones. The inn was recently sold and its future was uncertain at the time this book was printed.

The Old Orange County Courthouse is actually the fourth one built on this site. Captain John Berry built the current structure standing today in 1844. The clock in the courthouse is said to have been a gift from England, which originally hung in the first St. Matthew's church in London. This courthouse is one of the visual focal points of Hillsborough and adds majestic scenery to the town. There's always plenty of activity around the building with the Visitor's Center just down the street.

Corner cafés, gift shops, furniture stores, florists, antique shops, and hardware stores are just a few of the many varieties of merchants located in downtown Hillsborough.

Currently known as the Orange County Visitor's Center, *The Alexander Dickson House* originally stood about one and a quarter miles southeast of Hillsborough on the Occaneechi Farm. During the Civil War the house was the headquarters for Confederate General Wade Hampton. The outbuilding located behind the house was his very own office and General Johnston met with Hampton here in this office before setting out to meet Union General Sherman at the Bennett Place in Durham where terms of surrender were signed. The terms were signed on April 18, 1865 and ended Confederate Resistance in the South. This army was larger than the army that General Robert E. Lee surrendered at Appomattox. My family has passed the claim down through the years that General Johnston used the shirttail of one of my great, great grandfather's shirts as the surrender flag at Bennett Place. The house is a late 18th century farmhouse and has miraculously survived for over 200 years with only minor damage.

The Reverend Robert Burwell and his wife Margaret were two of the first people in the state to open a private school for girls. Used as the Presbyterian Manse by the Burwell's since Reverend Burwell was the minister of the *First Presbyterian Church*, they opened the school in August of 1837. The school specialized in history, mathematics, English composition, geography, art, music, needlework, Latin and French, and most of all, the study of Christianity. Sundays were spent worshipping and studying the Bible.

Mrs. Burwell became popular as a teacher at the School. It is said that she was even known as "the finest woman teacher in North Carolina." She not only taught school, but also had a large family, did gardening, church work and loads of household duties. One of the most noted educators to frequent the *Burwell School* was a Sicilian music master known as Signor Antonio di Martino. The house itself went through several enlargement periods. New wings and rooms were added throughout the years and Jule Gilmer Kerner (of whom the town of Kernersville was named after) was employed to renovate the house. Perhaps the most scenic feature of the old Burwell School is the garden and the grounds. Fruit trees, orange trees, sugar maple trees, elm trees, all sorts of flowers, hedges, ivy and a large vegetable garden are all testaments to Mrs. Burwell's fine gardening skills. In fact, some of these plantings still stand today. A bronze plaque marks an American linden, an Osage orange tree, and a huge 114-year old sugar maple tree, planted by Henry Brown in 1857. Brown had married a Burwell student and the family lived there for five years after the Burwells left to found *Queen's College* in Charlotte in 1857. *The Burwell School* is located on 318 North Churton St.

THE BURWELL SCHOOL

1837-1857

A project of the Historic Hillsborough Commission

The Orange County Historical Museum houses priceless artifacts dating all the way back to the pre-Revolutionary era. Seen here are flags, medical instruments, quilts, local silversmith items, old china, and the old pump organ used by the First Presbyterian Church.

Located in the *Confederate Memorial Building*, the museum was founded in 1956 by the Hillsborough Garden Club. The museum is supported by contributions from local and regional people and foundations, as well as the sale of historical pamphlets, books and maps. The museum is located at the corner of Churton and Tryon Street.

Seen here is a 160-year old working loom, a set of brass and copper English weights used by the town and dating back to 1760, and various flags, plaques, furniture and quilts.

Most of these items were donated by local townspeople, while some are on loan and imported from England and other towns.

Located just off I-85 at the Hillsboro exit is the famous *Daniel Boone Antique Village*. This is where antique dealers and collectors from all over the Southeast region gather to shop and trade every kind of item known to man. Years ago, a train (Blowing Rock's Tweetsie's rival) meandered through the area and local woods. It has since been closed down and sold.

The area was named after Daniel Boone who traveled through the area and helped establish the town. Here you will find antique shops galore, model cars, collectibles, old railroad cars, trading cards, firearms, and virtually anything else you're in the market for. Also here on location are many fine restaurants and a campsite with all the amenities.

Downtown Hillsborough not only contains many historic structures from the 1700's & 1800's, but also sports a beautiful line of storefronts made popular in the early twentieth century. One of the most notable structures is the *James Pharmacy Building*, which was used as a drug store up until the 1960's. The store now houses a popular deli known as *Lueg's*. Also in the building are several novelty shops located upstairs from the restaurant.

Another popular restaurant in the downtown area is the *Saratoga Grill*. Here diners are treated with window side tables on the second floor with wonderful views of Historic Hillsborough. Located in the same building are the charming *Court Square Shops*. Gifts, furniture, antiques and specialty items are featured in the shops located in this elegant turn of the 20th century building.

Even though Hillsborough is famous for its history, legendary buildings and archaeological significance, the town should also be recognized for its "Mayberry-like" hospitality and friendliness. Recently the town has become a popular destination for writers and employees from the universities at Duke and Chapel Hill.

Cobblestone sidewalks line the blocks of downtown, much like the sidewalks built in colonial times. Many historic markers such as this one honoring *Judge Edmund Fanning* are posted throughout Hillsborough.

Clean and smartly decorated sidewalks and streets accentuate the small town atmosphere created in *Downtown Hillsborough*. The area is breathtaking during the Holiday season when the town and historic homes open their doors for tourists to enjoy. The *Alliance for Historic Hillsboro* is an organization whose mission is protecting the history and culture of Hillsborough. Formed in 1991, the group is made up of six different organizations including the *Historical Society, Chamber of Commerce, District Commission, Historical Commission, Historical Museum* and the *Preservation Fund of Hillsborough*. These people are serious about keeping their town clean and authentic.

Built in 1816, the *Hillsborough Presbyterian Church* was the first church built in Hillsborough after the Revolutionary War. The original structure on this property was called *St. Matthew's Church of England* and it served as the *Provincial Congress* held here in town. It was built in 1768 and the *Constitutional Convention* was held there in 1788. Unfortunately the structure was destroyed by a fire in the 1790's. Located beside the present day building is the *Old Town Cemetery*. Many famous North Carolinians are buried in this graveyard. *William Hooper*, one of the signers of the Declaration of Independence; *Governor William A. Graham*, Secretary of the US Navy, US Senator, and Senator of the Confederate States; *U.S. Chief Justice Frederick Nash*; and *Colonel Archibald D. Murphy*, a state senator, war veteran, and also known as the "father of public education in North Carolina, are all buried in the Old Town Cemetery.

Known as the Ruffin-Roulhac House, *Hillsborough's Town Hall* is a stately colonial structure located at 101 E. Orange Street. Listed on the *National Register of Historic Places*, the building was first built in 1821. For the next 87 years several owners expanded upon the house. Martin Hanks, the original owner, built the west rooms in 1821. Then, in 1830 Mrs. Francis Blount-Hill bought the home and added the east rooms and the two-story hall. Chief Justice of North Carolina Thomas Ruffin bought the house in the 1860's and died ten years later in the northwest room. One of Ruffin's daughters married a Roulhac and the kitchen, observatory and pantry were added. However, in the early 1920's the house was tightly secured and stayed closed for over 50 years until the town began the rehabilitation of the house in 1974. Soon afterwards, the house was dedicated as the *Hillsborough Town Hall*.

Elkin

Growing up in a small community, sometimes your imagination leads you to new and adventurous places, but physically you never really get out of your own backyard. Northwest Forsyth County, where I grew up, is not quite country, not quite city. We lived right on the edge. If you drive west far enough on Highway 67, you go through several tiny communities. After some research on Surry County, I came across the little jewel that is Elkin, NC. Not only can you stop and shop on your drive up 67, you can also view several angles of the famous Pilot Mountain that juts out of the ground somewhere between Mount Airy and Elkin. Pilot Mountain is also known as Mount Pilot to Andy and Barney. Finally, after a pleasant little drive you see a bridge not too far away. Just north of Jonesville on the other side of the Yadkin River lies Elkin. The bridge that connects Elkin with its sister town Jonesville is rather impressive. A quick turn left once you cross the bridge lands you smack dab in the middle of a perfect little Mayberry, full of vibrancy, history and things to do. Elkin actually began in 1840 as a small manufacturing village and woolen mill by harnessing the power of Elkin Creek, and was incorporated in 1889. The railroad arrived in Elkin around 1890. Soon afterwards the town expanded as a result of commercial and industrial prosperity. Today Elkin thrives with many textile, agricultural and manufacturing facilities. Interstate 77 takes you right to it if you're trying to get there fast. Just remember to slow down once you get there. The average daily temperature is 36 degrees at its coldest and 77 degrees at its warmest. Not too cold, not too hot. The area offers advanced medical facilities, such as Hugh Chatham Memorial Hospital, an award-winning school system, arts and culture, and numerous recreational possibilities. The beautifully clean downtown area comes complete with gift shops, antique stores, art galleries (noted artist John Furches owns a gallery here), hardware stores and fine restaurants.

Downtown Elkin comes complete with shops, historic buildings and beautifully decorated sidewalks. It's a community with smiling faces on every street corner. It is also a thriving part of Elkin where locals and visitors take advantage of the convenience and atmosphere.

In business since 1911, The Elkin Tribune operates out of its own impressive structure on Main Street. The paper serves the Elkin/Jonesville area as well as Stokes, Wilkes and Yadkin Counties . Downtown Elkin has a program where local merchants and businessmen have gotten together to make the area more appealing to prospective new businesses and residents. Nine new businesses, including two art galleries, an antique shop, a health club, and a children's shop have each opened within the past two years. The area is growing, but remaining true to its own small town ideals.

Pilot Mountain, the majestic monolith that rises out of the ground somewhere between Winston-Salem & Mount Airy, is extensively photographed and painted. You can see many different angles and views of the mountain on your trip to Elkin. *The Andy Griffith Show* used the name of the mountain and switched it around for the fictitious town of Mount Pilot. The Elkin Parks & Recreation Department offers many community activities including youth softball & baseball, pee-wee flag football, swim teams, summer day camp, junior team tennis and youth basketball. One particularly popular annual event in Elkin is the Yadkin Valley Pumpkin Festival held the fourth Saturday in October.

Many inviting, quaint restaurants and coffee shops are located downtown. The Elevator Café is located in one of the first buildings ever built on Main Street. Erected in 1895, it was used as a grocery store up until the 1930's when a hardware store took over. Now a popular restaurant, it serves as a testament to the fact that the people here in Elkin are proud of their town and its heritage.

Snow-covered hills add to the picturesque qualities and the down-home feeling of Elkin. These pictures were taken in March after a late-winter snow that took place. Elkin Creek flows past Galloway Church and flows into the Yadkin River. Built in 1898, Galloway Memorial Episcopal Church is the oldest church in town still used for regular worship services.

The Yadkin Valley line, whose tracks first brought business and commerce to Elkin, still delivers freight, merchandise and passengers to the area. Many towns in North Carolina would not have developed at all were it not for the railroad. By helping build small towns, the railroad companies practically shaped and molded an entire nation.

The Elkin-Jonesville Bridge is an impressive structure, which sprawls across the Yadkin River between the two towns. Great views of Elkin are visible when crossing over on the bridge. Other routes are available, but this approach is the most attractive.

Elkin has managed to survive through the Great Depression, floods and fires. The fact that Elkin Creek and the Yadkin River come together here in town led to the foundation of civilization in the area. Elkin's most prosperous industry has been wool. Founder Richard Gwyn moved here from just across the river in Jonesville in 1840 to establish a wool manufacturing company.

Located right beside the Foothills Art Council, this building, known as the *Richard Gwyn Museum*, was built in 1850 by Gwyn (the town's founder) to be used as a church and school so that his family would not have to travel to Jonesville for worship and education. It is the oldest building in Surry County ever used as a church or school. It was converted into a museum in 1953.

When Richard Gwyn moved from Jonesville he settled on the
north side of the Yadkin River. He soon realized the potential of
Elkin Creek. He and his family harnessed the power of the creek
by building a dam and used that power to manufacture grist, run a
smithy, a sawmill, a cotton mill, and in 1851, a general store. Today
the dam stands as a tribute to Gwyn and his family, as well as being
one of the beautiful scenic spots in Elkin. The town is well aware
of its small town allure and characteristics. The citizens work hard
to preserve that charm and are quick to speak highly of Elkin's
wonderful appeal.

The Hugh G. Chatham Bridge was built in 1931 and is 1,509 feet long. It serves as one of the connectors between Elkin and Jonesville by spanning across the Yadkin River.

There is nothing like good, ole country cooking. Located just outside East Bend, O-Henry's is a very popular place to stop on Highway 67 on your route to Elkin. It's also quite the hangout in the mornings at breakfast time for all types of people, including the fishermen on their way out to the Yadkin.

Most of the buildings located on Main Street in Downtown Elkin were constructed after a fire in 1898, which completely destroyed the majority of frame structures. A man named R.L. Poindexter built many of the existing buildings from brick. These two story buildings are decorated with panels, round-arched windows and painted brick. This type of construction was popular in the early twentieth century and there are few remaining towns like this in the Northwestern part of the state.

Royall's Soda Shop, located in the first floor on 128 West Main Street, has been serving up delicious hot dogs, burgers, shakes and ice cream since 1924. Notice the electric train in the picture below while the ladies are hard at work preparing lunch for some lucky customers. Royall's is not to be missed. On the second floor Elkin's first hospital was established. In its first year the facility admitted 350 patients. This proved the need for a bigger hospital, which was built in 1931 as Hugh Chatham Memorial Hospital.

   The hustle and bustle of Downtown Elkin breathes life into the town that offers plenty of Mayberry nostalgia. Elkin is so close to so many attractions. Located only a few miles from the Blue Ridge Parkway and right off Interstate 77, the town attracts tourists, and recent retirees alike. For those who need a small town to call home while still being centrally located, Elkin is just the place. An hour from Charlotte, forty minutes from Winston-Salem and thirty minutes from Statesville, Elkin fits in perfectly for the city dwellers looking for escape and release from the pressures of everyday life.

Davidson

Have you ever imagined living in a charming, Mayberry-esque village where you can get anywhere you need to go, on foot? Davidson, NC is such a place. With a population of just over 4,500, it is estimated that one out of four citizens either works at home or walks to work. With Davidson College being the town's main centerpiece and employer, it should come as no surprise that the town is culturally and educationally influenced, as well as well-kept. In fact, some of the buildings on campus are on the *National Historic Register*. Established by a group of Presbyterian clergymen in 1837, Davidson was named after General William Lee Davidson who was a local Revolutionary War hero. Known then as "Davidson College," the town was incorporated in 1879 as the "Town of Davidson College" before being officially changed to "Davidson" in 1891. Davidson College employs over 500 faculty members and staff, is one of the leading four-year liberal arts institutions in the country, and is absolutely essential to the life of the town. Davidson has been described as a safe and happy place to raise a family or retire to. The town is also home to Dr. Thomas P. Clark. Dr. Clark is a former Professor of Religion at Davidson College and famous for his gnome sculpting. By 1985

his popularity had grown so much that he retired from teaching and began sculpting on a full-time basis. Many of his pieces have become collector's items and are quite valuable. Davidson boasts beautiful brick sidewalks, streets lined by trees and hanging baskets, and some of the finest shopping, eating and scenery any small town can offer. While strolling down the picturesque village sidewalk, one can find an old-fashioned soda shop, gift and book stores, a clothing store, a florist, a retirement community, an art gallery among others, and a busy little café where residents congregate to read the paper and talk over a cup of coffee. But most importantly, one will discover smiling faces, old-time hospitality, and genuine friendliness. Quaint neighborhoods, town homes and condominiums are close-by. Annual events to look forward to include "Christmas in Davidson" where the town is elegantly decorated and the shops on Main Street open up together to ring in the season, and the NCAA Soccer Tournament, which is held on campus. Whether you're in town for a visit or looking to relocate, Davidson is the perfect place to relax and enjoy the warmth and peacefulness of small-town life.

This elegant late 19th century brick house is now home to two fine Davidson merchants. *The Needlecraft Center* and *Piccadilly Hairdresser & Colourist* are located within the walls of this beautiful structure, complete with a rocking chair front porch and some amazing landscaping.

Established way back in 1951, *The Soda Shop* here in Downtown Davidson is a landmark and a perfect little place to grab a quick bite. Located next door is *Classic Bride*, a bridal shop with a wide selection of dresses and accessories. Local shops flourish in Davidson where local citizens and merchants know how to appreciate the charm and benevolence of small-town life.

The Town of Davidson is kept clean and beautifully decorated with hanging baskets, flowerpots, charming shops & storefronts. Trees line the streets and an incredible brick sidewalk adds to the relaxed atmosphere this town generates. Many different types of restaurants are located in the downtown area. There's a soda shop, a French bistro, a deli & café and a Ben & Jerry's. The service at these restaurants immediately brings to mind the Bluebird Diner on The Andy Griffith Show, friendly and helpful.

The shops in Davidson offer a wide variety of choices to meet any need. Book shops, clothing stores, all kinds of gift shops, art galleries, framing shops, flower shops and antique stores are all complete with good old fashioned hospitality and kindness. Davidson is a peaceful and intellectually stimulating town, fit for young and old alike.

The *Davidson Parks & Recreation Department* organizes and sponsors many events and recreational pastimes including soccer, softball, tennis, karate, dance classes, baseball, basketball and swimming. Davidson is very much a place where families get together and enjoy all types of activities. It's a neighborly place where friends help friends and groups of people gather for cookouts, church softball games and Boy and Girl Scout meetings. Being close to *Lake Norman*, Davidson has many water sports to offer including skiing, wave boarding, boating and just plain cruising the lake. *Lake Norman* is not only easy to get to from Davidson, but also provides some beautiful scenery.

One of the most predominant and noticeable structures in the town is the stately *Davidson College Presbyterian Church*. The town of Davidson was founded by Presbyterians who moved into the region in the 1700's. Attending church service on Sunday was a requirement of all students up until the 1970's. Nearly one-fourth of the students at Davidson regard themselves as Presbyterians. The church can hold up to 1200 people.

The streets in Davidson are lined with many historic homes. Some of these are used as bed & breakfasts, including *Harris Farm Bed & Breakfast, The Davidson Village Inn* and *The Lake Davidson House Bed & Breakfast*. The *Davidson Walking Tour* is perhaps the best way to explore these unique & magnificent structures.

Gatherings like this cookout by the water are very common in Davidson. The town has many popular annual events in which local citizens play an enormous part. One such event is known as Town Day. This is held on the first Saturday in May when Main Street is blocked off and the heritage of the town is the focus of the celebration. There are tons of rides and games for the kids. Churches and civic organizations set up booths and sell some fabulous home-cooked food. The infamous egg-drop contest takes place and concerts and raffles are held as well. A huge, old-fashioned parade takes place every Fourth of July, which comes with homegrown watermelons. The Children's Schoolhouse Carnival is held in the fall on the village green, complete with rides and games. As the holiday season gets closer, the town of Davidson is filled with the magical, friendly and festive feeling of Christmas spirit. The town dresses up for the occasion and literally travels back in time to create many wonderful events to brighten holiday sprit. Norman Rockwell comes to mind. Many stores have their own musical entertainment and stay open a little longer. Groups of carolers stroll the beautifully decorated streets. Surprise visits from Santa spring up throughout downtown. There's even a dog fashion show and to top it off, three nights of enchanting and captivating carriage rides.

What small town Christmas celebration would be complete without a parade? And what a fantastic one it is! Floats, marching bands, clowns, horseback riders and of course, Santa himself. Davidson really knows how to celebrate Christmas.

A view of Main Street shows an attractive & picturesque village where people are quick to smile and say hello. Students enjoy a relaxed atmosphere as they huddle over their books in the delis and outdoor cafés. People take walks through the beautiful Davidson College campus with no fear and the evening sun brings a lazy Sunday afternoon to an end.

The Village Store on Main Street is a unique and old-fashioned little gift store. All kinds of decorations and accessories are available including wind chimes, pottery and lamps. Most of the storefronts on Main Street are located opposite the college and offer splendid views of the campus.

The *President's House* (seen here) is a fine example of 19th century architecture. Note the beautiful Roman columns in the front and the hanging front lamp. Ancient oak and elm trees, some over a hundred years old, are located in the front yard. Another famous home in Davidson is the Carnegie Guest House. Built in 1910, the house was originally supposed to have been a library, but instead was converted into a guest house used to entertain visitors, as well as prospective students and their families. In the past the house was also used for social functions by college organizations.

A peaceful stroll through the Davidson College campus upon the many paved walkways leads you through some incredibly scenic and relaxing settings. The trees create a cool shade on a hot summer day and the lawn is always a beautiful shade of green and very well kept.

The main entrance to Davidson College, located on Main Street, is handsomely decorated with flowers and shrubbery. Known for its focus on liberal arts, the college currently enrolls nearly 1,600 students. The campus is 450 acres of beautiful scenery, historic brick buildings and architecture where learning is complete with a relaxed atmosphere.

Davidson College brings life, vitality & enlightenment to the town of Davidson. The college is famous for providing education and cultural enrichment to students in the arts including drama, dancing, music and painting. The Davidson College Visual Arts Center holds exhibitions of the works of students and The Davidson Community Players Summer Theatre is famous for its annual professional dramatic presentations.

The *Village Cupboard* is a charming little deli and café located on Main Street. The restaurant also has its own wine & gift shop, so you can eat and shop in one place. It specializes in delicious sandwiches and a variety of coffee flavors. Add to that a patio under the awning out front and some rocking chairs along the brick sidewalk and you've got a great place to relax and take in the fresh air. Perhaps scanning the morning newspaper with a fresh cup of java on a cool Saturday morning is more to your liking. Whatever your pleasure is, the town of Davidson aims to please.

Mount Airy

"Mayberry, my hometown," that's how most of us Andy Griffith Show fanatics describe the hometown of our TV hero, Andy Griffith himself. Griffith called Mount Airy "home" from his birth in 1935 up until 1966 when he moved his aging parents out of their house on 711 Haymore Street to live in California to be closer to him. While Andy swears up and down that Mayberry was not based on the real-life town of Mount Airy, there is evidence against that claim and we fans like to think otherwise. Located at the foot of the Blue Ridge Mountains and only a few miles from the Virginia border, Mount Airy began in the early 1750's as a stagecoach stop between Salem, NC and Galax, VA. The town soon took its name from a nearby plantation bearing the same moniker. The village had been well known as Mount Airy for nearly 70 years before it was incorporated in 1885. The town developed largely due to its huge granite quarry, textile industry and furniture manufacturers. The town was named one of 1994's All-American Cities and was voted as one of the top 100 best places to live in the United States. Mount Airy plays host to the annual pilgrimage for Andy Griffith Show fans. The "Mayberry Days" festival has been held here on the last weekend of September for the past 14 years. People flock from all over the country to tour the town and collect memorabilia. Located in the middle of downtown are several landmarks mentioned on the show, including Snappy Lunch, Floyd's City Barber Shop, Wally's Filling Station & The Bluebird Diner. Visit the Andy Griffith Playhouse and Andy Griffith Homeplace, as well as the Mount Airy Visitors Center, where you can view the largest collection of Griffith artifacts in existence. Everything from old comic books to Otis Campbell's actual wardrobe is on exhibit at the Visitor's Center. I must mention, however, that there's a lot more to Mount Airy than just Andy Griffith. There's Bluegrass, Barbeque, Historic Homes, Ice Cream Socials, Festivals of all kinds and I don't know what all.

Many of the local retail stores like the *Surry Art Market* (shown here) carry a variety of Mayberry souvenirs. From pictures to t-shirts & coffee mugs, if you can put Andy Griffith on it, they've got it. Today tourism is by far the largest economic provider for the town of Mount Airy.

Perhaps the smartest place to begin your journey is here at *The Mount Airy Visitors Center* (above). The most impressive display of Andy Griffith memorabilia known to man is on display in the Visitor's Center. The center itself is housed in a stately restored house on Main Street just a few blocks away from downtown.

Mount Airy is a small town lover's dream. The ambience and atmosphere of a Mayberry-like setting is intact, while all the modern conveniences of a big city are minutes away. Mount Airy is famous for several annual celebrations including Mayberry Days, The *Autumn Leaves Festival, Downtown Tales* and *The Bluegrass & Old Time Fiddler's Convention*. The town has all kinds of antique & gift shops, furniture stores, art galleries, hotels and bed & breakfasts, jewelry stores, book stores, clothing outlets, hardware stores, movie theatres, restaurants, and of course, a barber shop.

Home of the Surry Arts Council, *The Andy Griffith Playhouse* began life as the site of the first public school in Mount Airy. Built in 1920 and known as *Rockford School*, the building underwent a major renovation in 1975 when the Arts Council rented it and turned it into the impressive theatre and arts center that it is today. In fact, Andy Griffith attended Rockford School and even performed on the stage. It was named after Griffith in the early seventies. The Surry Arts Council is responsible for scheduling its annual events and extensive activities that take place throughout the year. From bluegrass concerts to plays, musicals, award ceremonies and everything in between, the Playhouse is fully equipped to accommodate various types of events. Bluegrass jamborees, in particular, are extremely popular here at the Playhouse. Perhaps that's because of another Mount Airy legend by the name of *Tommy Jarrell*. Jarrell is a bluegrass innovator and legend whose fiddle is housed in the *Smithsonian Institution*. Other famous Mount Airy natives include country singer *Donna Fargo* and *Eng & Chang Bunker*, the longest surviving conjoined twins in the world.

Made famous by The Andy Griffith Show, *Snappy Lunch* has been a staple in Mount Airy and an institution since 1923. Owner Charles Dowell, who started working here in 1943 sweeping floors, has gained nationwide fame for his one-of-a-kind pork chop sandwich. It's a generous portion of delicious pork, fried to perfection and served on a bun. Andy Griffith often frequented the restaurant as a young boy living in Mount Airy. These days finding a seat in the restaurant is as hard as finishing off one of Dowell's delicious sandwiches.

Driving north on Highway 52 the beautiful sight in the distance is the Blue Ridge Mountains. In fact, the mountains are only minutes away from Mount Airy. The Blue Ridge Parkway, which meanders through several states is easily accessible from Mount Airy just a few miles up 52. Mountain culture and pastimes such as bluegrass, pottery & quilt making are very prominent and important in Mount Airy.

Barney Fife ate countless meals at the *Bluebird Diner*. In fact, he was dating Juanita the waitress on the side, even though Juanita was never seen on the show. The diner is located in the heart of town and features fabulous home-cooked meals and is famous for making incredible milkshakes. It is one of the first Andy Griffith Show landmarks you notice as you drive into town on Main Street.

Located at City Hall is an impressive replica of the courthouse and jail (below) seen on The Andy Griffith Show. *The Mayberry Jail* was used for municipal purposes at one time and the jail inside was an actual holding area for desperate criminals. The car is also a recreation of "the squad car" used on the show. It's extremely popular with tourists who come to Mount Airy looking for the actual Mayberry. Tours of the jail are available; while rides in the patrol car are only allowed in emergency purposes, or for going to the store for groceries. *Wally's Service Station* (above), located off Main Street just outside of downtown, is also a replica of the garage used in the show. As usual, water and air are free, but they do make a charge for gas and oil.

It's also a popular place to pick up a bottle of pop.

The *Andy Griffith Homeplace*, one of the many charming bed & breakfasts in Mount Airy, is located less than a mile from the downtown area. The Griffith's purchased the house way back in 1935 and sold it in 1967. Andy lived there up until the time when he went off to college at *the University of North Carolina at Chapel Hill*. A local businessman bought the house in 1998 and then sold it to the owners of the *Mount Airy Hampton Inn*. It officially opened as a bed & breakfast in 1999 and is currently being operated by the owners of *The Carriage House Bed & Breakfast*. It stays pretty booked up as you can imagine. Mount Airy has several other charming bed & breakfasts. Each one is unique in its own way, but all are true to an earlier way of life. Some of these include the *Mayberry Bed & Breakfast*, the *Merritt House Bed & Breakfast* and the *Pine Ridge Inn*. The town is also fully equipped with full service hotels for visitors including *Best Western Bryson Inn, Callaway Motel, Comfort Inn, Hampton Inn, The Hollows Motel, Knights Inn Motel, Mayberry Motor Inn* and *the Star-Lite Hotel*.

Commerce in Downtown Mount Airy is alive and well with all kinds of stores including furniture, antiques, restaurants, movie theaters, clothing, books, hardware, drug stores and practically anything else you can think of.

It is estimated that Mount Airy tourism has gone up more than 430% in the last ten years. Many attribute the increase to the popularity of the Andy Griffith Show and the annual Mayberry Days celebration. In addition, a non-profit group of local business owners and civic leaders known as *Downtown Mount Airy, Inc* has played a major role in the renovation and marketing of the downtown area. The most important part of Mount Airy, and any small town for that matter, is the fact that the people are friendly, helpful and always willing to help out a neighbor with smiles on their faces. Local citizens work hard to keep the town clean, authentic and Mayberry friendly.

Located beside *Snappy Lunch* is another Andy Griffith haunt seen most frequently on the show. *Floyd's Barber Shop*, renamed Floyd's after the show, the barbershop is a favorite stop for The Andy Griffith Show fans of all ages. Owner Russell Hiatt has been working there for over 50 years. He still remembers the last time he cut Andy's hair. And as usual, there are 2 chairs and no waiting.

Local Mount Airy residents take great pride in keeping the downtown area clean. Early 20th century storefronts line Main Street and side streets such as Pine Street. Even though there are some of the larger retail stores close by, most prefer to do their shopping downtown where they can find anything they need.

In addition to having a popular and exciting downtown area, Mount Airy also has a large number of historic homes in the district. Some are even on the *National Register of Historic Places*. The town is fully equipped with all the modern conveniences of hospitals, a great school system, community projects and much more. Also, some wonderful restaurants in the area include the *Wagon Wheel Restaurant, Gaunce's Cafeteria, Leon's Burger Express, The Derby Restaurant, Aunt Bea's Barbecue, O'Dell's Sandwich Shop & Drive-In Restaurant, Pandowdy's, Brintle's Restaurant* and *The Dairy Center.*

Located directly across from the *Mount Airy Post Office* is this eye-catching *Veterans Memorial* with an impressive fountain and landscaped area. This was erected in honor of all the local veterans in Mount Airy. J.E.B. Stuart, the Confederate general who fought beside General Lee in the Civil War, was born about six miles north of Mount Airy. His birthplace is now the site of an annual Civil War reenactment in October. Stuart was born on the property known as Laurel Hill in February of 1833.

Another popular attraction in Mount Airy is the outlet stores. These include the *Cross Creek Apparel Outlet, Homeway Furniture Outlet, Pine State Knitwear & Sweater Outlet* and *Renfro Sock Store & Outlet.* There are several beautiful historic homes in Mount Airy including the *William A. Moore House, Gertrude Smith House* and *the Edwards-Franklin House.*

Southport

Quietly tucked away on the North Carolina coast within an hour of Wilmington and Myrtle Beach lies the historic and wonderfully preserved fishing village known as Southport. Widely popular for its scenic beauty and small-town charm, Southport has served as a protection harbor and vantage point since the days of the pirates in the mid-1700's. Its streets are lined with ancient oak trees, waterfront shops and restaurants that echo a time when life was slower and friendlier. Today Southport still has that feeling of friendliness and peacefulness, but the town is also flourishing with over 15 antique shops, art galleries, a wide variety of restaurants, the *Southport Maritime Museum,* historic homes and sites, and some beautifully scenic waterfront parks. Although the Spanish explored this area in the early 1500's, the town was not actually created until 1792. Pirates used the harbor in the early 1700's and the notorious pirate Stede Bonnet was captured in the harbor in 1718. The North Carolina General Assembly commissioned five men to put together a town called Smithville, named after Benjamin Smith who served under George Washington in the Revolution and later was elected Governor of North Carolina. Smithville became the county seat of Brunswick County in 1808. In the 1880's a push for the town to become a major Southern port took place due to the railroad and the shipping industry. Therefore the name was changed to Southport. Unfortunately, those plans never fully reached their potential and the county seat was relocated to a town nearby called Bolivia. A walking tour is recommended for those who love historic sites and homes. Beginning at the Visitor's Center, this walk through town visits the *Indian Trail Tree* in *Keziah Memorial Park,* estimated to be over 800 years old, Franklin Square Park, *City Hall,* built in 1854, the *Hubbard House* built in the 1850's, the *Brunswick Inn* circa 1859, and the *Adkins-Ruark House* built in 1890. These, along with the charming downtown area, are just a few of the many sights to behold. Perhaps the most breathtaking piece of scenery is *Waterfront Park,* complete with a whittler's bench, a fishing pier, views of Bonnet's Creek, the Cape Fear River, the Intracoastal Waterway; and finally, spectacular views of Oak Island, Bald Head Island, and Battery Island, a wildlife refuge. Included in the views of the islands is the Bald Head Island Lighthouse and Oak Island Lighthouse, both spectacular and majestic pieces of architecture. Historic Fort Fisher and Fort Johnston are also both close by. The film industry located just north in Wilmington has also discovered the picturesque beauty of the town.

Many motion pictures including scenes of "Crimes of the Heart", which featured Diane Keaton, Sissy Spacek, and Jessica Lange were filmed in Southport. In addition, the popular television show "Dawson's Creek" has had several scenes filmed in the town. So, when you're on vacation at the beach, or looking for a place to call home, the lovely town of Southport has everything you could possibly need to experience small-town atmosphere and benevolence.

The Southport Trail is a self-guided walking tour complete with map and illustrations of Historic Southport. *The Southport Historical Society* sponsors the tour. There are many historic homes on the walking tour. These include the *Adkins-Ruark House,* built in 1890, where noted author Robert Ruark spent many of his summers as a child.

Also on the walking tour is *Historic Fort Johnston.* Named after Governor Gabriel Johnston, the fort was the first one commissioned in North Carolina. The brick building, known as the *Garrison House,* was erected in 1805. The fort was destroyed by North Carolina militia in 1775, thus ending British government in the state. It sits right at the mouth of the waterway where the Cape Fear River meets with Bonnet's Creek. This provided safe haven for Southport for many years. Today the fort is the smallest known working military site in the country.

Other historic homes included in the tour are: *The T.M. Thompson House,* built in 1868 and owned by the successful Civil War river pilot Captain Thomas M. Thompson; *The Hubbard House,* built in the 1850's; *A.E. Stevens House, built in 1894;* and the *Walker-Pyke House,* built in 1800 and the oldest surviving house in Historic Southport.

The *Keziah Memorial Tree* is a sight to behold. It is estimated to be over 800 years old. The tree was bent by the Cape Fear Indians to be used as a marker on a trail. It was named after a popular local newspaperman named Bill Keziah and is a unique part of Southport's history. In 1715 there were many Indian villages in the Southport area, but by 1720 the European settlers had taken over. The tree itself is actually located right around the corner from the Visitor's Center.

Bull Frog Corner is a wonderful gift shop, full of stuffed animals and all kinds of specialty gifts. Be sure to visit all the little shops in downtown Southport, including, *Basketcases-Gourmet Food & Specialty Gift Baskets, Bull Frog Corner, Candy Bouquet of Southport, The Christmas House, Driftwood Shell Shop, Etcetera, Mangoes, Prince of Brunswick, Waterfront Gifts & Antiques* and *Party Time – Hallmark*. Shopping in Southport proves to be extremely relaxing and enjoyable with gentle saltwater breezes and beautiful scenery to behold.

Where else can you get information on history, shipwrecks and discovered artifacts? You go to the *North Carolina Maritime Museum* in Southport. Look for the Jolly Roger flag hanging off the side of a historic brick building on Howe Street and you'll discover an amazing variety of memorabilia and collections from Southport's historic past. A helpful self-guided tour is available. Museum guides are on duty to answer questions. The informative storyboards that line the museum walls are expertly constructed and researched. Satellite photos of the area, Civil War artifacts including a torpedo, golden crosses, diving helmets, shark teeth, countless shells, model ships, whale bones, and some of Gentleman Pirate Stede Bonnet's writings are all part of this impressive display at the museum. A research library and classroom complete with videos is set up to provide information for presentations and study. Hurricane tracking is also covered in depth. Located conveniently in the downtown area, the museum is one of the most popular stops for people visiting Historic Southport.

The Southport Visitors Center is located one block from the waterway in the heart of downtown. Centrally situated on the corner of Howe and Moore Streets, it is the starting point for an exploration of Historic Southport. This incredible timeline in the building covers the history of the town from it's early beginnings as an Indian Village to a present day thriving vacation destination. Bed & Breakfasts including *Almakecon Inn, Brunswick Inn Bed & Breakfast, Cape Fear Inn* and *Lois Jane's Riverview Inn* are all charming accommodations in Southport. Information is also available on the many annual events such as the North Carolina 4th of July Festival where arts & crafts booths are set up, live entertainment, food, things for the kids and so much more are on hand. Another popular event is the Christmas By The Sea Festival. The downtown merchants decorate their storefronts and the sidewalks with ornaments, mistletoe and seashell ornaments. A tour of the historic homes in Southport is available along with a lighted boat parade and the shops stay open just a little longer to get all that last minute shopping in before Santa pays his visit. Of course, Southport wouldn't be Southport without seafood. There are many fine restaurants serving up some wonderful coastal cuisine including *Barb's Seafood & Midtown Deli, Dry Street Pub & Pizza, Famous Subs & Pizza, Fish Factory Restaurant, Lucky Fisherman Restaurant, The Pharmacy Restaurant, Sandfiddler Restaurant, Ship's Chandler Restaurant, Shrimp House Restaurant* and *The Trolly Stop.*

Large, stately oak trees line the city streets and flowerpots and benches are lined up and down the sidewalks. Strolling through the area brings a laid back and relaxing state of mind to people visiting and living Southport. The area is thriving with specialty, antique and gift shops. Coffee houses such as the *Café Bean* offer delightful settings to sit and enjoy an impressive variety of coffee flavors and treats.

When you need a break from the shopping be sure to pay a visit to the Whittler's Bench down by the waterfront. Since 1898 people have gathered at this popular site to catch up on the latest gossip or to discuss the next social gathering.

There are many convenient parks to add to an already extensive list of things to do in Southport. *Caviness Park Franklin Square Park, Keziah Park, Riverwalk Park, Stevens Park, Waterfront Park, Lowe-White Memorial Park, Southport City Gym, City Pier* and the *Southport Community Building* are all part of the Parks and Recreation Department. They offer everything from tennis courts to baseball fields.

Many of the shops, art galleries and restaurants are located in old historic homes and buildings. This is evident in the many extraordinary Victorian homes and buildings preserved in the downtown area.

Many spectacular antique stores thrive in Historic Southport. With so many different stores, shopping is peaceful and fun. These stores include *Prince of Brunswick, Northrop Antiques Mall, Southport Antiques, The Curiosity Shop, Back 'n Time, The Helmsman, Magnolia Gifts & Antiques, Second Hand Rose,* and *Glass Menagerie Antiques*. Southport is fully equipped with retirement communities like Sacred Heart Villas and modern medical facilities to help in emergencies. With a population of less than 3,000, it's no wonder people from all over are flocking to this extremely charming waterfront village.

Located almost directly across the street from the *Southport Visitor's Center* is an absolutely stunning Victorian home that has been converted into one of the most unique shops in Southport. *The Christmas House* stays decorated for the holidays throughout the year and houses some of the most beautiful decorations in the South. Inside the house, Christmas trees are all decked out. Ornaments, nutcrackers, snowmen, ribbons, bows, bears, Santa Clauses, maritime decorations, books, snowflakes and virtually anything you can imagine pertaining to the season are strategically and beautifully decorated. An electric toy train chugs through the store on an elevated track and a gazebo sits out front to allow weary travelers and tired shoppers a place to sit, relax and enjoy refreshments. The Christmas House is a "must-stop" for all ages.

Perhaps the most popular park in Southport is *Waterfront Park.* Located on Bay Street at the end of Howe Street, the park is a vantage point where views of the Bald Head Island Lighthouse and the Oak Island Lighthouse are clear and photogenic. The Oak Island Light is the brightest lighthouse in the country and the second brightest in the entire world. From the park you can also smell the salt air and see the many ships that pass through the waterway on their way to destinations across the sea. Covered picnic tables and benches are available and parking lots provide convenient places to stop and enjoy the views.

Another popular thing to view in Southport is art. The town boasts many unique art galleries including *The Art Shak Gallery, Blue Crab Blue, The Franklin Square Art Gallery, the June Gottlieb-Brown Studio, Justine Fine Art & Crafts, The Ricky Evans Gallery, Shade Tree Gallery* and *The Southport Art Gallery.* Many other fine local merchants in Southport include *Davis Dry Goods, Hilda's, Isabella Grape, Ropa, Etc., the Good Ship Lollipop, Books n' Stuff, Rebecca's Fabrications* and *Cape Fear Jewelers, Ltd.* Southport is a one of a kind small town with perfect surroundings, atmosphere and above all, people.

Beautiful Harker's Island, Shackleford Banks and Carrot Island can all be viewed from the waterefront.

Beaufort

One of the first towns I thought of when my idea for this book came to mind was the peaceful, little waterfront town of Beaufort. I'd visited the place numerous times throughout my life. My aunt lived in Atlantic Beach/Morehead City for many years and our family had eaten at *The Net House* on a regular basis. The town is quietly tucked away between the Bogue & Core Sounds. Beaufort's charm, beauty, history & heart brings to mind Charleston, SC. Yet Beaufort has a personality all its own. Settled in 1700, Beaufort is North Carolina's third oldest town. The downtown area and cemetery are both on the *National Register of Historic Places* and the streets are named after many of the English Royalty of the early 1700's. Incorporated in 1723 and named after Henry Somerset, the Duke of Beaufort, the town has been the Carteret County Seat since its beginning. Beaufort boasts several bed & breakfasts, art galleries, museums, walking tours, double-decker bus tours, boat tours, shops, restaurants and a waterside boardwalk perfect for strolls after dinner. Benches line the boardwalk for those of us who eat too much seafood at dinner or enjoy "boat watching." Close by is a wildlife refuge where wild ponies roam free, a pre-Civil War fort (Fort Macon), Atlantic Beach, and ferries departing to Ocracoke and Cape Hatteras. Renovated homes dating back to pre-Revolutionary times line Front Street by the water while the shops & restaurants in the downtown area beckon the antique or souvenir collector in all of us, not to mention the hungry sailor yearning for some of the finest seafood or steak in the world. Special yearly events include Publick Day/Colonial Market Day (3rd Saturday in April), Old Homes Tour & Antiques Show & Sale (last weekend in June), Community Thanksgiving Feast (Sunday before Thanksgiving), and the Coastal Carolina Christmas Celebration (Second weekend in December). Watch out for pirates. Many colorful characters are known to frequent the small harbor town on a regular basis, but don't be afraid. They wouldn't harm a flea. Visit Beaufort anytime of the year for a pleasant, enjoyable and educational experience.

The Dock House is well known as one of the most popular spots in Beaufort to spend time, enjoy food, drink, and most of all, scenery. The restaurant overlooks the waterway and boats parade by regularly. On occasion there is also a musician performing Jimmy Buffet tunes to add to the already relaxed atmosphere.

Many of the old historic buildings in the downtown area now serve as antique and gift shops like the *Turner Street Emporium* and *Beaufort Antiques*. Downtown Beaufort projects a certain waterfront charm and atmosphere straight out of the early twentieth century.

Walk down the busy streets and enjoy the calm, cool breezes coming in off the water. Beaufort has a comforting effect on everyone. You've also come to the right place if you're looking to shop, dine in excellent restaurants, sightsee, go fishing or boating, or just explore the incredible history of Beaufort. There are several special group tours of Downtown Beaufort available at group rates. Some of these include *Old Burying Ground Tours, English Double-Decker Bus Tours in the Historic District, Architectural Walking Tours* and *Special Civil War Bus Tours*. All of these tours are offered through the *Beaufort Historical Association*.

One major attraction for visitors in Beaufort is *The North Carolina Maritime Museum*. The museum houses numerous exhibits, including model ships, shells and many displays of historical shipyard and seaworthy artifacts. There are also plenty of classes, lectures and programs available for young and old alike.

Beaufort is located only a short drive away from the Crystal Coast. Emerald Isle, Indian Beach, Salter Path, Pine Knoll Shores and Atlantic Beach are all very popular vacation destinations and offer spectacular beaches & restaurants. *Fort Macon State Park, the North Carolina Aquarium* and the *Core Sound Waterfowl Museum* are some of the attractions in the Beaufort area.

Clawson's Restaurant (shown here) and *The Net House* are among the celebrated seafood restaurants in Beaufort. The architecture of the Clawson's building is reminiscent of early 1900's classic storefront structures, which adds to the magic of the town.

The town is a favorite docking destination of boats from all over the country. Walking along the waterfront dock in Beaufort is a popular pastime. Beaufort is well known for its pleasant hospitality, beautiful scenery, fine seafood and laid back atmosphere.

This row of houses on Front Street reminds you of Charleston, SC. However, Beaufort has a charm all its own. Some of these well-preserved homes date back to the early 1700's and the street names are taken from British Royalty. Names like Ann Street, Queen Street, Moore Street and Craven Street are all derived from royalty from that time period.

Located in Historic Beaufort are some of the most delightful bread and breakfast inns in the state, many of which are sitting right on the waterfront. *Elizabeth Inn, Captain's Quarters, The Carteret County Home Bed & Breakfast, The Cedars Inn, Cousins Bed & Breakfast, Delamar Inn, Langdon House,* and *The Pecan Tree Inn* are all included on this fine list. *Finz Grill and Eatery, Loughry's Landing, The Sandbar Restaurant, Spouter Inn Stillwater Café, Clawson's Restaurant* and *The Net House* are restaurants that offer a wide variety of some of the most amazing seafood you'll ever taste.

Beaufort was the home to the legendary pirate Blackbeard. Not only did he own a house in town, it is said that his ship went down not far from here. In fact, efforts to recover the sunken vessel are currently a hot topic in Coastal North Carolina. Tours of Blackbeard's house, known as "Hammock House" are available. Some of the other famous historic buildings include the *Carteret County Jail* built in 1859, *Samuel Leffer's Cottage* built in 1778, the *Rustell House* built in 1732, the *Carteret County Courthouse* built in 1796, the *Apothecary Shop & Doctor's Office* built in 1859, the *Joseph Bell House* built in 1767 and the *Josiah Bell House* built in 1825. Another popular tour in Beaufort is *The Old Burying Ground*. Listed on the *National Register of Historic Places*, many of the graves date back to the early 1700's.

There are nearly 100 historic homes and buildings in Beaufort, too many to mention in this book. These homes display extremely unique and masterful architectures. Notice here the wrought iron fence and beautiful brickwork. The pointed roof on this three-story masterpiece reflects Victorian charm and elegance. Beaufort takes great pride in preserving the artifacts of yesteryear. There's a strong sense of community here, along with an attention to detail when it comes to cleanliness and upkeep.

Several well-kept gardens live behind historic homes and in hidden alleyways in Beaufort. Many of these can go unnoticed. But luckily, there are plenty of tour guides who know all about these secret gardens.

What began as a small fishing village on *Taylor's Creek* is now a safe haven for the person seeking a slower, laid-back lifestyle. Boat tours are available, as well as fishing excursions. The *Big Rock Blue Marlin Tournament* is held annually in the area. In fact, pretty much all the water sports are represented here in Beaufort including water skiing, jet skiing and scuba diving.

The *General Store* is a living testament to Beaufort's preservation efforts. At the store you can enjoy hand-dipped ice cream, do some laundry, pick up today's paper, buy a gallon of milk or a box of nails. The general stores were the main shopping spot for people years ago. Maybe that is why so many flock to these memorable stores. Perhaps they come to steal a glimpse from the past or maybe to see what life was like before the world became so generic. Today the General Store is still a place where anything and everything is sold.

Below is a partial view of downtown and Front Street. The streetlamps you see light up the village at night and create a captivating ambience and feeling. Nightlife is popular in Downtown Beaufort. A convenient parking area is provided on Front Street near the waterfront dock. Beaufort is so much more than just shopping and dining. It's a place where people come to loosen up and let their cares go.

A good place to begin your tour of Beaufort is here at the *Beaufort Historic Site* where artifacts from the town are on display, local artists demonstrate their work, and wedding receptions take place on the grounds. While you're there, visit the *Robert W & Elva Faison Safrit Historical Center* and *The Old Beaufort Gift Shop* at the site. *The Beaufort Historic Site* is located at 138 Turner Street, just a few blocks up from the waterfront and docks.

Wild horses roam the nearby deserted islands looking across the water from Beaufort. Luckily, these unspoiled wonders are now protected from commercial development. One of these, *Shackleford Banks*, is a natural wildlife sanctuary and was also a playground for some of North Carolina's most notorious pirates. In fact, the entire area was teeming with pirate activity back in the 18th century. Beaufort is located a few miles west of Morehead City. Morehead City is equipped with modern medical facilities, retirement communities, suburban neighborhoods and industry.

In addition to all the wonderful things you can discover at the *Beaufort Historic Site*, you can take the double-decker bus tour, which allows you to see the entire town, the waterfront, and enjoy those salty air breezes from an open-air bus.

The storefronts in Downtown Beaufort are absolutely beautiful. Well-designed and crafted architecture and decorated sidewalks help create the laid-back and relaxed shopping atmosphere that the town is so proud of. Discover gift shops, antique stores, furniture stores, clothing outlets and fine restaurants. It's easy to make a day of it in Beaufort. Everything you need is well within walking distance.

The waterfront dock provides a tranquil visual walk for the fisherman, the boating expert, the pirate, or for walking off that huge plate of seafood. Beaufort provides the ideal small town coastal feeling for the person who wants to get away from it all.

Swansboro

It's no wonder that this historic, shipbuilding village is best known as "The Friendly City by the Sea." If you're looking for a place to slow down, Swansboro is the perfect town to do just that. Located just across the bridge from the highway 24 & 58 intersection (just down the road from Emerald Isle), this wonderfully preserved, waterfront town has everything the doctor ordered for shopping, dining, lodging, boating, fishing, or just plain relaxing. The elegance and charm of the downtown area pays homage to the dedicated local citizens who strive so hard to keep it nice, clean, and under-commercialized. The history of Swansboro dates back to the early 1730's. The first settlement began on this former Indian village right where the White Oak River runs into Bogue Sound. Named after the then speaker of the North Carolina House of Commons, Samuel Swann, the town was incorporated in 1783. The building of ships became the biggest industry in Swansboro and the small, but popular port city grew stronger. In fact, Captain Otway Burns constructed North Carolina's very first steamboat, the *Prometheus*, here and the village continued its growth until the end of the Civil War. After the war, the lumber industry gained prominence, but soon after the Depression, the town's citizens turned to the sea and commercial fishing proved to be the best way for Swansboro to survive. Take a stroll through downtown and you'll find gift & antique shops, eye-catching art galleries, inviting restaurants with spectacular waterfront views, and smiling faces as you walk by. Some exciting annual events include the Storytelling Festival, the Mullet Festival, Arts-by-the-Sea, and the Christmas Flotilla. Just up the road on highway 58 is the noted Crystal Coast Amphitheater where "Worthy Is The Lamb" is performed from June 18th - September 18th. This world-class outdoor drama is second to none in its reproduction of Jesus' life and times. Extensive research was done in order to recreate the biblical story and scenery as accurately as possible. A must see for visitors.

For a different atmosphere on the waterfront try *Yana's Restaurant*. Decorated in authentic 1950's style, this exciting restaurant serves up fine seafood, burgers and old fashioned ice cream and shakes. To complete the atmosphere, a Wurlitzer Jukebox cranks out favorite tunes from the fifties.

Duck Crossing combines antiques and books with a country store –type building to create a unique shop. It's only one block away from the waterfront.

Swansboro is centrally located between Topsail and Emerald Isle. What started as a small shipping and fishing village is now a thriving destination for tourists and retirees. The downtown area is full of all kinds of shops and restaurants all within walking distance of each other. It has been said that if you are looking for a copy of the *Wall Street Journal* in Swansboro, you'll be lucky to find one that is less than two weeks old. It's a relaxed and laid-back town with plenty of fun to offer.

There are many restored homes for rent in Swansboro. Many of them are only a block from the waterway and rent for weeks and even months at a time. Several charming bed & breakfasts are located near the historic district. These include *Scotts Keep Bed & Breakfast, Sunrise Lane Bed & Breakfast, The Harbor Light Guest House* and *Mount Pleasant Bed & Breakfast.*

A spectacular view of the Swansboro Bridge is on the waterfront as you shop *Kristi's Gallery,* which is a popular shop featuring local and regional artisans. Other popular galleries in Downtown Swansboro include *The Phil Shivar Gallery, The Tidewater Gallery* and *The Art Master Gallery.* Swansboro is a popular destination for vacationers needing a break from the beach. The town is across the water from the stretch of sand known as "the Crystal Coast." This includes Atlantic Beach, Salter Path, Pine Knoll Shores and Emerald Isle, all just minutes away from beautiful Historic Swansboro.

From the *Harbor House deck*, you get spectacular panoramic views of not only the waterway and bridge. Also, the whole town can be viewed, including *Port O' Swansborough* where shoppers flock. *Harbor House* is known as a marvelous gift shop, as well as a nice place to relax with a little dessert.

    Swansboro has more than its share of antique and gift shops. Be sure to visit *Lighthouse Antiques, Inc., Brass Binnacle, Swansboro Antique Center, American Sampler, Gray Dolphin, Noah's Ark, Remembrances II, Ferrands, Russell's Olde Tyme Shoppe, Sunshine & Silks, Through the Looking Glass, River Emporium General Store & Fudge Co., The Barber Shop Antiques & Collectibles* and *The Silver Thimble Gift Shoppe*. Also located in Swansboro are jewelry & clothing stores such as the *Lighthouse Boutique, Vilinda's Sportswear and Golden Traits Jewelry*. Most importantly, the merchants and residents are well aware of the importance of tourism to their town and really do go out of their way to make you feel relaxed and at ease. Smiling faces greet you wherever you go and the warm sea breezes coming off the water are very calming and peaceful.

Just a few blocks away from the business district is a historic residential area. Houses built in the late 1800's and early 1900's are kept neatly decorated by their current residents. People sit on front porches and drink afternoon tea while kids of all ages stroll along the sidewalks.

As you walk through this wonderful little town, be careful not to step on any ducks that may be walking along with you. *Bicentennial Park* is close by and that's usually where they are headed. The park is a popular place to do some duck feeding.

Standing on the deck at the Harbor House Gift Shop and looking over to the right is a wonderful view of the stores on Front Street. One prominent feature is the elegantly restored brick building known as *The Olde Brick Store* (below). Located inside this impressive structure is one of the most unique maritime and shipping shops in the state, known as *The Brass Binnacle* This fascinating store specializes in authentic marine artifacts and reproductions. Everything from clocks to portholes and model ships are featured, as well as lighthouse models and items to decorate with the coast in mind.

One popular spot to grab a bite is the *Church Street Deli*. Sample some gourmet coffee and enjoy delicious homemade ice cream just yards away from the waterfront. You may decide to sit back and relax on the porch in one of the many rocking chairs. In the background is the water tower and many of the gorgeous historic homes.

Another popular tourist attraction is *Hammocks Beach State Park*. A short boat ride to Bear Island brings you face to face with sea turtles and beautiful unspoiled beaches. Sand dollars and wonderfully colored shells are all at your fingertips here in this wildlife-protected island where nature is king and humans are scarce.

Located in a beautifully restored home, *Lazy Lyons Antique Shop* offers the finest in collectibles including furniture, decorative lamps and pottery.

The famous *Russell's Olde Tyme Shoppe* takes you back in time with a wide variety of beautiful and charming gifts and accessories. Right down from Russell's is *Noah's Ark*, an adorable little shop with everything from unique jewelry to puppets and metal art. Notice the nostalgic wooden structures that line Front Street.

Front Street is a shopper's paradise with so many different types of charming and friendly shops. *The Silver Thimble* is popular for its variety of collectible thimbles from all over the world; as well as a vast array of music, teapots and sets, and old-fashioned toys of all kinds.

A splendid variety of outdoor activities are available here in Swansboro. There are boat charters, camping grounds, fishing piers, golf courses, RV parks, scuba diving and all sorts of water sports to choose from. Perhaps your favorite outdoor activity will be to take a seat on one of the many park benches and relax while enjoying a wonderful view of the seagulls, waterway and neighboring islands. With all of these activities to take in, including the shopping; you can expect to build up quite an appetite. Not to worry, Swansboro is home to many fabulous restaurants. These include *The Fish Trap, Captain Charlie's Restaurant, The Church Street Coffee House, The Gourmet Café, Yana's Restaurant, The Flying Bridge Restaurant, White Oak River Bistro, Riverview Steak & Seafood, The Hummingbird Café* and *Kings BBQ & Chicken, Inc.* Swansboro is a special place to come when relaxing and shopping is on top of your list. It is also special to the local residents who love it so much. It has been said that you can leave your door open and unlocked without any fear. There's something to be said about a place where worry is non-existent and taking it easy is a way of life.

CONTACT INFORMATION

Dillsboro

Contact Jackson County Travel & Tourism Authority at 828-586-2155,
or write to 116 Central Street - Sylva, NC 28779
For more information on all the wonderful options on the Great Smoky Mountain Railroad visit www.gsmr.com.
For further research and exploration be sure to visit www.nc-mountains.com, www.visitdillsboro.com,
www.dillsboromechants.com and www.mountainlovers.com.

Black Mountain

Contact the Black Mountain Chamber of Commerce at 828-669-2300,
or write to 201 East State Street, Black Mountain, NC 28711
For more information visit www.blackmountain.org, www.exploreblackmountain.com, or www.blackmountaincollege.org.

West Jefferson

Contact the Ashe County Chamber of Commerce at 888-343-2743,
or write to PO Box 31, West Jefferson, NC 28694
Also, visit www.ashechamber.com.
For a full schedule of all the wonderful events going on at the West Jefferson Arts Center be sure to call 336-246-ARTS.
Lost Province Tours, call toll free at 888-877-4480, or visit www.fastransit.net/lptours.

Mount Olive

Contact the Mount Olive Chamber of Commerce
at 919-658-3133, or write to 123 N. Center Street, Mount Olive, NC 28635
Tours and information about the Mount Olive Pickle Company are available by logging on to www.mtolivepickles.com.
Also, visit www.moachamber.com and www.mountolivetribune.com.

Liberty

Contact the Liberty Chamber of Commerce
at (336) 622-4937, or write to Post Office Box 986, Liberty, NC 27298
Visit www.visitrandolph.org and www.libertyjubilee.com for more information.

Hillsborough

Contact the Orange County Visitor's Center at 919-732-7741,
or write to 150 East King Street, Hillsborough, NC 27278
To learn more visit www.hillsboroughchamber.com, www.ci.hillsborough.nc.us and www.historichillsborough.org.

CONTACT INFORMATION

Elkin

Contact the Greater Elkin-Jonesville-Arlington Chamber of Commerce at 336-526-1111,
or write to 116 East Market St., Elkin, NC 28621
Visit www.ejachamber.com, www.elkinnc.org, and www.elkinnc.com
for more information.

Davidson

Contact the Davidson Visitors Center at 704-892-2447,
or write to 305 North Main, Davidson, NC 28036
To learn more go to www.ci.davidson.nc.us, www.davidson.edu, www.lakenormanchamber.org.

Mount Airy

Contact the Greater Mount Airy Chamber of Commerce at 336-786-6116, or 800-948-0949
or write to 200 N. Main Street, Mount Airy, NC 27030
For further information be sure to log on to www.mtairyncchamber.org, www.visitmayberry.com and www.mtairynews.com.

Southport

Contact the Southport 2000 Visitors Center at 910-457-7927
or write to 107 E. Nash Street, Southport, NC 28461
To find out more visit www.southport-oakisland.com, www.insiders-southport.com,
www.oak-island.com and www.oldesouthport.com.

Beaufort

Contact the Beaufort Historical Association at 919-728-5225,
or write to 138 Turner Street, PO Box 1709 - Beaufort, NC 28516-0363
Visit www.blackbeardthepirate.com, www.beaufort-nc.com,
and www.historicbeaufort.com for further information.

Swansboro

Contact the Swansboro Area Chamber of Commerce at 910-326-1174,
or write to 502 Church St., Swansboro, NC 28584
Go to www.tourswansboro.com, www.nccoastonline.com/TidelandNews.html,
and www.crystalcoast.com/swansboro/sponsors/ for further information.

IN CONCLUSION...

It is becoming more and more apparent that in this day and age, small towns are important to this nation's values, ideals and beliefs. Their sense of innocence and their benevolent settings bring to mind a simpler, more relaxed way of life that is missing in today's hectic and dangerous world.

Taking into consideration the lessons taught on *The Andy Griffith Show* and applying them to our everyday lives can send us searching for something more out of life. Perhaps it is time to slow down a little and take some time off from the things that stress us out so much.

In this book I tried to highlight a small few of North Carolina's special and wonderful towns. A small town can be a place to spend a vacation. It can be a destination for some fabulous shopping and restaurants. It can be a place to relax, get away from it all, go hiking, take a boat ride, tour a museum or enjoy an outdoor bluegrass concert. Perhaps a small town can even be a place called "home."

Maybe you're recently retired and ready to find a place where people call you by name and offer to help you plant that garden you've always wanted. Maybe you're searching for a safer place to raise a family, where you can leave your front door unlocked and not worry about your children playing in the neighborhood. Maybe you live in a city and need a way to relax and relieve some stress. I hope that this book has provided an outlet for all these things and more.

Just because you don't live in a small town doesn't mean that you can't flip through this book and appreciate the goodness and tranquility of small towns. As I stated earlier, there are more than 120 small towns in North Carolina that are similar to that mythical, magical and wonderful town we all know and love... Mayberry.

Enjoy your search, and as Gomer would say,
"lots of luck to you and yours!"

– Scott